CK00 705417

Mbarara Genesis

Early European Travellers in Ankole and the Founding of Mbarara by an African, Asian and European Initiative

David Weekes

Lavender Inprint
London

Published in 2014
by Lavender Inprint
235A Rotherhithe Street, London, SE16 5XW
to whom any communications should be addressed by e-mail:
lavender.inprint@gmail.com

First printed in parts between 1973–1980

First published in this format 2014

The Reverend David Weekes
asserts the moral right to be the author
of this publication.

Copyright © David Weekes

ISBN 978-0-9565501-4-9

Other titles by the same author include:

The Origins of Lexham Gardens and Lee Abbey in London
(1995)

A Short Description of Kilmany Parish Church (2009)

A Short Guide to Kilmany Churchyard, Fife (2009)

ΧΡΙΣΤΟΣ ΝΙΚΗΣΕΙ On John Buchan's Grave (2010)

How Captain James set Churchill on the Path to Glory (2010)

What Sir William Fettes Really Meant (2010)

Kilmany in Fife: Glimpses of History (2013)

This book is dedicated
with all love and gratitude
to our family members
who shared the Ankole experience
from 1969–1973:

Jean
my wife, sometime teacher at Ntare
and Headmistress of the *Boma* School

Richard and Catriona
in their early years, and
Robin
who joined us three months after it ended;

also to honour the memory of
James Sonco Bwogi Tumuhirwe
recently of Ntare School, Mbarara
when he was murdered
among friends
by agents of President Amin
September 1972
and his generation of Ntare men
others of whom also perished

CONTENTS

ILLUSTRATIONS

ACKNOWLEDGEMENTS

Every writer's family suffers, and most of all I thank the members of mine who are honoured in the dedication. In addition I have cause to be grateful to many other people over the last forty-five years. Without the prior labours of all the writers of letters, memos, reports, journals, articles and books, I could not have written anything of this. In Uganda there were still others like Richard Pelham White, a colleague at Ntare who gave me encouragement then, and those among the clergy at St James's Cathedral, Ruharo who generously allowed access to the records there. The staff of the Libraries at the University of Makerere and The Uganda Society were always most helpful; Professor Bryan Langlands at Makerere gave further encouragement, and first published some of this material; the then Curator of the Archives at Entebbe readily provided much assistance with material there and enabled the copying of Macallister's letter. When on leave in 1971, there were the daughters of the Reverend Herbert Clayton, some or all Mbarara born, and three of whom entertained me in Kendal, who were quite extraordinarily generous and trusting in lending me the metal biscuit tin containing all the letters and photographs sent from Mbarara to their grandparents (this was at a time when they had not yet been copied elsewhere), and allowing me to use them over many months. Back in Britain I received much help with primary sources from those then at the Archives of the Church Missionary Society and of the White Fathers' House in London, as well as at the Libraries at Lambeth Palace, the Royal Commonwealth Society, and at Rhodes House in Oxford; the Reverend Brian McAllister gave personal information and gifted the photograph of his father. Long ago Miss Grant in the vicinity of Turi in Kenya did the typing of a long draft at a critical time, and very recently Ernest P. Clark, Jr. of St Mary's College in the University of St Andrews has, with infinite patience, kindly assisted greatly in preparing the final text for publication. Some others are acknowledged in the following pages. In such a list, ranging over so many years, there are bound to be unintended omissions; my thanks are no less sincere to any others who feel that their names should have been included.

ILLUSTRATIONS

All such material here is out of copyright, but due acknowledgement is made, and with warm thanks to those responsible for providing any kind of help with these illustrations. Both covers have reproductions photographed from within watercolours by Anna Dudley (Mrs Michael Neill), a contemporary and friend in Mbarara, and the design is by Ernest Clark. Maps 1 and 2 are by the author; Map 3 is taken from the folded one in Jack's book; for Map 4, made and signed by Macallister, see below note 290; 'A Woman Taken', 'Ntali's Gift' and 'A Slave Caravan' were drawn by Major Casati and are from his book, pages 278, 279 and facing 290; Stanley is from his *Autobiography*; Igumira is from J. F. Cunningham's book page 11; the Group of Ankole leaders, and the K.A.R. soldiers are from Johnston's book Vol.II, pages 633 and 641 (there is a considerable difference in indigenous clothing in other photographs of his compared with those of Cunningham taken a couple of years later); 'Mbarara Headquarters' comes from Garstin's *Report*; 'Katwe Fort' is from a watercolour by Bishop Tucker reproduced in his Uganda reminiscences, Vol. 2, facing p.130; Map 5 (the Site Plan of Mbarara) and Map 6 (Major Cunningham's Journey), are by the author and from his articles in the *Uganda Journal*Clayton is courtesy of his family; Galt has been extracted from a group reprinted in *Uganda Journal*; 3/3 (1936) facing page 240; the postmarked Rowling is courtesy of the late Roy Dunstan; an extensive search for a photograph of G. G. Cunningham has not yielded any result so far.

I

PREFACE TO THE PRESENT EDITION

Three papers, first published well over thirty years ago form the basis of this book. Whatever their inadequacies, they were pioneering work on the origins of the town of Mbarara in Western Uganda. If for no other reason, in each case typographical inaccuracies in the process of printing justifies bringing them all together within one cover to provide a better version of what I had first written. Two of them appeared as articles in *The Uganda Journal* Volume 37 (1973). After a regular run of forty years this issue proved to be the last before only occasional volumes appeared thereafter. Because it was produced during a period of great political upheaval and violence in Uganda, it only finally came out in 1975 as a result of the patience and perseverance of the late Professor Bryan Langlands of Makerere, and those who helped him. While they were acutely aware of the number of errors in the text when it appeared in print, they had no control over them.

These misprints sometimes confused the discussion, and destroyed the identity of some of the place names. I attempted to counter these inadequacies by sending a corrected copy to the University of Nairobi. Nevertheless, these articles are much more likely to have been read in the adulterated form over all these years.

The fieldwork in Uganda for the first two articles reprinted here was done under singularly difficult and restricting circumstances between 1969–1973. Unwittingly, however, I was particularly fortunate in applying for access to the old Secretariat Archives at Entebbe shortly before the military *coup* which ousted President Obote in January 1971. I received my permit soon after that in a brief period of greater openness before restrictions became ever tighter. Without such access these first two articles could not have been written. It is possible that some of those sources no longer exist.

With the army in control, travelling about was restricted and asking questions became grounds for suspicion. Nevertheless as an Anglican clergyman I had been able to meet with Canon Yoweri Buningwire, and Mr Lazalo Kamugungunu, a former *Enganzi* of Ankole, both of whom had been among the early converts to Protestant Christianity, as well as with Mr A. G. Katate, a long-standing Catholic. The last two of these had collaborated jointly in writing their own historical account in the vernacular. The Right Reverend Kosiya Shalita, then Bishop of Ankole, and Dr A. C. Stanley-Smith who had been a C. M.S. missionary in those parts for more than fifty years did much to provide local information and encouragement.

Then on returning from Uganda to Scotland in 1973 I continued to enquire into the background of Macallister, the founding Sub-Commissioner, who remained a sketchy figure in what else had been published by that time. Since he was not a university graduate, or prominent enough for an entry in *Who's Who* either, there was no ready source of biographical information. However, once I had established that he was the son of the Reverend John M'Allister (surname spelling varies) of Plumstead, the *Alumni Oxonienses* revealed that his eldest brother was the Revd W. M. C. McAllister, for many years Vicar of Hempstead in Norfolk. A letter to the incumbent led to correspondence with a parishioner who gave me the address of the former Vicar's nephew. This was the Revd B. R. McAllister, the only son of the Mbarara pioneer. He was now retired, and died soon after my correspondence with him. Perhaps because we were both ordained to the ministry of the Church of England, and he had no immediate heirs, he very generously gave to me his father's commission from the Imperial British East Africa Company and from Queen Victoria as Vice-Consul in Uganda, together with photographs of him (the originals have unfortunately since been destroyed by fire).

For personal interest in 1974 I wrote a long, unpublished paper entitled 'Language, Literature and the Bible in Ankole.' This forms the basis of Chapter Nine. A few years later I was asked to provide an understanding of Macallister's background for an article in the *Bulletin of the East Africa Study Circle,* a rather obscure, and as far as I know short-lived, journal. Despite the philatelic context, this subject has a surprising bearing on the founding of Mbarara township through the activities of the first Protectorate Sub-Commissioner (administrator-in-charge). It is included within these pages and gives useful additional information about the background and personality of the man who was himself so prominent in the administrative endeavour (see especially Chapters Three to Five & Appendix B). This last of the three published papers appeared in an England without excuse, and yet contained a conclusion opposite to that which had been submitted for publication. Reprinting also gives an opportunity to add something to the maps originally included with the first two, and the illustration accompanying the text of the third.

Over the years since then I have been fully engaged in other matters. It is unlikely that I shall have further opportunity for research into the history of Ankole, and of Mbarara in particular. My contribution to these fascinating topics is therefore limited to what I wrote many years ago, and is contained in what is reprinted in this volume and in my thesis. This is entitled 'The Growth of Christianity in the Kingdom of Nkore (Ankole), in Western Uganda Before 1912' (University of Aberdeen 1979). Hopefully it will soon be published as *Ankole Religion and Christianity.* There I enquire further into the religious background which played such an important part in stabilising the altered political situation from the 1890s onward. Included there is a further discussion of the initial encounters between Europeans and the traditional kingdom of Nkore which is begun in Appendices A & C in this volume. These early journeys established the first contacts between the European outsiders and the indigenous people.

Now having more leisure at the end of a busy working life, I have thought it useful to publish these various pieces together. One article from *The Uganda Journal*, is scattered through a number of chapters while the other is reprinted as Appendix C; it is relevant to the Mbarara story because it was through this journey that the location of "Ntali's" and "Muti" became known to Europeans; that from the *Bulletin of East Africa Study Circle* is the basis of Appendix B. Appendix A inevitably touches on some of the information given earlier, but it is an attempt to provide a full list of the Europeans who came to any part of Ankole between 1876–1901, to indicate their route and their purpose. In order to treat them as human beings rather than heroes or villains, something more about them and the rest of their lives will be found in *Ankole Religion and Christianity*

It is natural that I should dedicate this book to my family, but also to the memory of James Tumuhirwe. I have the most vivid memory of him as the prefect on duty in the dormitories before lights-out in Aggrey House. He presented a somewhat fearsome figure – a little stubble on his chin, and carrying a staff, but wearing his Scouts uniform. In point of fact he was a gentle, intelligent boy, understandably puzzling over the world about him and trying to come to terms with it. Soon, while on vacation from Makerere, it was his misfortune to be staying with a school friend whose father was targeted by Amin. James perished with the household, and very sadly became one of the innocent victims of that brutal period in which Uganda lost so much of its potential.

Kilmany, Fife, October 2014   DW

I had no purpose in such writing except to please myself, and even if my books had not found a single reader I would have felt amply repaid.

John Buchan in *Memory Hold the Door* (1940) p.196.

REFERENCE CODES FOR CMS AND ESA ARCHIVES

Footnotes in the following pages contain many references to the archives of the Entebbe Secretariat (ESA) of the former Protectorate, which are now part of the Uganda National Archives, and also to those of the Church Missionary Society (CMS). These references were noted long ago and some, or all, of the class marks may have since been changed. No doubt the staff at these essential primary sources will be able to give guidance.

GLOSSARY OF LOCAL WORDS

Nkore The traditional name before 1898, thereafter it was known as Ankole District, but consistency is difficult since the Anglicised form was in use earlier.

Banyankore People of Ankole

Bahinda Ruling clan

Bahima Cattle people

Bairu Agriculturalist people

Runyankore (Lunyankole) The language of Nkore (Ankole)

Omugabe "King" of Nkore (Ankole) – honorific prefix *Rubambansi*

Enganzi "Prime Minister" – honorific prefix *Owekitiinisa*

orurembo *Kraal* of the *Omugabe*

omukago The act of making Blood Brotherhood

Baganda People of Buganda, sometimes *Bagonya*

Luganda   Language of Buganda

Kabaka   "King" of Buganda

Katikiro   "Prime Minister"

Saza   A territorial subdivision within the kingdom of Buganda often described as a county, with its *Saza* Chief. Like some other *Luganda* words it was adopted in Ankole.

Bakoki   People of Koki

Omukama Another *Bantu* equivalent of "king" used in Bunyoro, Toro and Igara

Batoro   People of Toro

Rutoro (Lutoro) Their language

Banyoro   People of Bunyoro

Runyoro (Lunyoro) Their language

Askari   *Swahili* for soldier

Baraza   A place of public meeting

Kraal   An enclosure for human habitation (usually in huts) and their cattle

Muzungu (Mzungu) The usual term for a white man

Shamba   A piece of cultivated ground

Zeriba   A protective fence of thorn

It is questionable whether there should be an in initial 'o' in words like *Omugabe* (rather than *Mugabe*) and *omukago* (rather than *mukago*). The former spelling has been widely used, especially perhaps by Europeans and by the first *Banyankore* historians, and is adopted here. The more recent writer, Dr Karugire, tends to the latter, but not always consistently in writing his history (1971), though more so in *Mbaguta* (1973). Later still Dr Kagume uses the former, which is adopted here.

Apart from proper names, vernacular words should usually be found here in italics.

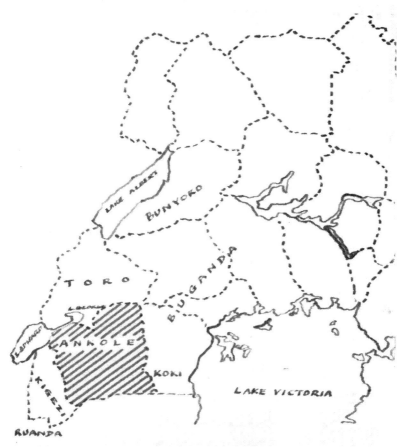

Mbarara Genesis

MAP 2. TRADITIONAL NKORE WITH ANKOLE DISTRICT

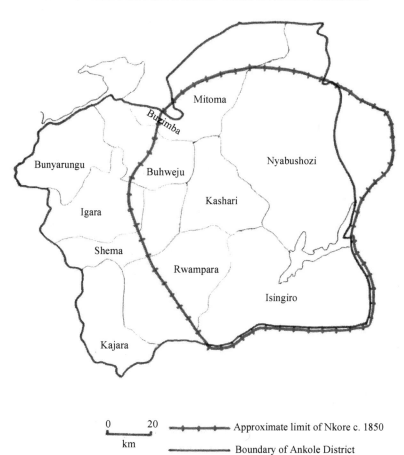

| 0 | 20 | ⊢+◆+◆+◆+◆+◆+ Approximate limit of Nkore c. 1850 |
| km | | ━━━━━━━ Boundary of Ankole District |

MAP 3. MBARARA IN THE CENTRE OF ANKOLE

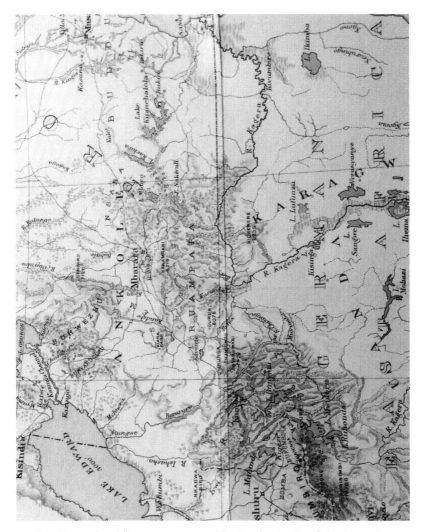

The first scientific map surveyed by Major Jack of the boundary
Commission in 1907 (turn clockwise to view)

MAP 4. MACALLISTER'S ANKOLE 1900

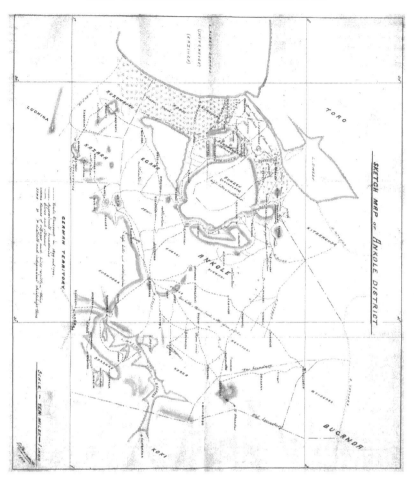

Hand drawn and signed by the Sub-Commissioner
(turn anti-clockwise to view)

CHAPTER ONE

EXPLANATION AND INTRODUCTION

The word "Genesis" simply means beginning, creation. This first word from the Old Testament in the Bible seems especially suitable for inclusion in this title. Moreover, the creation of Mbarara was also really out of nothing, as we shall see. Those who began the process by which Mbarara has evolved, whatever their differing motivation may have been, were all in some way stepping out in faith that something better could be achieved for the future. "God made from one all nations to dwell on the earth" (*The Acts of the Apostles,* chapter 17 verse, verse 26) and despite the rivalries and jealousies which keep peoples apart, happily there are many examples of those who work together in a common purpose.

Therefore it is a pity that historians have often written about primary collaboration with the transitory colonial power, or primary resistance to it. There has been a tendency to denigrate the former and champion the latter as though those who stuck rigidly to the traditional life were engaged in an heroic endeavour. However, had primary resistance triumphed there would have been no progress. At the end of the nineteenth century the inhabitants of Nkore were still living an age-old traditional pastoral and agricultural life. Perhaps in a tropical environment it was not greatly different from the lives of many communities in Europe in the recent past. However, it lacked any literature, and had experienced none of the scientific advances which had characterised the West since earlier ages.

Guns, unhappily, were among the first of these to be introduced. They were brought by foreigners in the 1840s, for by the early nineteenth century Arab settlements on the east coast of Africa had become "an overseas empire subject to Oman." These then encroached on the interior where

Slaves and ivory – the black gold and the white – were the

objects of quest that first took the Arabs to the populous regions around the great African lakes, for in their opinion no other trade was sufficiently lucrative to justify the expense of such arduous journeys.[1]

Europeans are often blamed for the Slave Trade, and they were certainly most culpable in the transportation overseas. However, that evil would have been impossible without the prior iniquity of Africans capturing their fellows, and passing them on to Arab traders. They in turn enslaved them, and marched them to the coast to sell on. All three races seem equally to blame for this nefarious practice, though Britain was ultimately foremost in seeking to end it. The Royal Navy was long active in suppressing the trade at sea, though the financial cost of doing this was high, but it was still rampant on land and waited to be confronted by other means, as will be seen, see below p. 20. This is how the trade in slaves continued to work:

> Though commonly known as 'Arabs' the slavers were usually coastal *Swahili* with a slight admixture of Arab blood. Their methods were insidious and certain. The slaver would enter his chosen district as a peaceful trader, posing as a friend and using every means to gain the confidence of the local tribes. To all appearances he was himself a chief: liberal and wealthy, surrounded by armed followers (*ruga-ruga*); provider not only of coveted trade goods but also of those instruments of authority and power, firearms and powder. In such circumstances the slaver had no difficulty in securing adherents. The next move was to participate in the perpetual local quarrels. With every advantage on their side the *ruga-ruga* could not fail to win, and it was natural enough that their master should exact his toll of slaves from the defeated enemy. To conduct raids for the express purpose of securing slaves now followed easily, and so the long caravans to the coast began.[2]

Arab slavers had not only brought such weapons but also new diseases which were devastating the people. Outsiders had brought these ills and only other aliens could effect a cure. Inevitably the West would somehow also encroach upon tradi-

---

[1]   Moyse-Bartlett, H., *The King's African Rifles*, Aldershot (1956) pp. 3–4.

[2]   *Ibid*, p. 7.

RAIDING. 'A woman stolen'

tional life in Nkore, and its people would be brought fully into contact with the wider world. In the case of Uganda it was Britain, though with much reluctance, which proclaimed the Protectorate in 1894 in order to prevent the Belgians or the Germans from doing so, as well as to curtail this trade in slaves. Some have been glad that it was not one of these other nations that did so.

It can be argued that the colonial period was an inevitable interlude, a bridge over which Ugandans passed from the old to the new, from the age-old traditional life to full participation in the contemporary modern world. At the height of Idi Amin's repression older inhabitants of Mbarara would say reproachfully, "Why did you go away? You left us too early, and we were not ready." Others with more perception would say, "You must forgive us, you had your Henry VIII." That very apt remark showed an understanding of the capricious brutality of that monstrous king's reign about which in the present day many of his countrymen are unaware. Those who said those things to me had no lingering romance about the benefits of primary opposition.

As we look back, it is easy to underplay the great amount of initial primary acceptance of the Colonial Administration, and to forget that this was extended to embrace Nkore by invitation of the kingdom's authorities. Moreover, once this outpost had been established it was 'held' in its earliest days by only four Europeans, one half Irish, another from Ireland and two who can be assumed to have been English. They were accompanied by a company of Sudanese troops, likely to have been little more than a hundred strong,[3] under the command of the two English. It is difficult to avoid the conclusion that any concerted primary opposition could have made life very difficult for such a small foreign presence, but there was no violence in the Mbarara vicinity. Dr Karugire is undoubtedly right to stress that any opposition tried to ignore what was happening in the vain hope that the Europeans would go away.[4]

Thus it came about a few years later that the founding of the modern town of Mbarara resulted from international co-operation of the kind that has already been applauded. Without the involvement of the various races the early development would have faltered, and then foundered altogether.

The site above the Ruizi river had first been chosen by indigenous African leaders in time immemorial. They were itinerant cattle people who used it spasmodically, but had abandoned it for the time being. It awaited the arrival of those from overseas, and in particular British administrators, for a permanent settlement to develop there into a modern town.

Naturally many of the people of the locality, the *Banyankore*, were much involved, while natives[5] from other parts

---

[3]   They were attached to the Uganda Rifles, and incorporated into the King's African Rifles in 1902. Prior to the First World War the total strength of the K.A.R., not including officers, was 2,325 men. The three battalions (only one of which was in Uganda as the continuation of the Uganda Rifles) were divided into twenty-one companies. Therefore each company consisted of only about one hundred and ten men. These companies were at the pre-war size known as 'half-company strength' which is why there are some references to half companies in official correspondence.

[4]   Karugire, S. R. *Nuwa Mbaguta*, Kampala (1973) p. 73. Both Stanley and Casati were in no doubt about the determined and aggressive attitude shown by the people of Nkore compared with others they had met, *In Darkest Africa*, London (1890), Vol. II pp.347-348, and Casati, G., *Ten years in Equatoria*, London (1891) pp.273, 279-280.

[5]   'Native' should not be thought to be a derogatory term. In *ibid*, p. 63,

of Uganda and from further afield were also employed in the process as the first soldiers and police, or in other ways. Asians contributed some of the building skills and were engaged in trade. Of course, all this was not achieved by any detailed pre-arranged accord, nor was it in any way inevitable, but unfolded pragmatically as individuals were prepared to work with strangers, sometimes against the prejudice of the majority of their fellows. The openness towards others shown by these pioneers, however haltingly and imperfectly expressed, is a challenge for our later generation to emulate, and in so doing also to achieve great things. This book is written in celebration of what can be achieved through such united endeavour.

It is now forty years since my family and I left Uganda, and this book is best read as though it was published a few years later in about in 1980.

The author retains a deep affection for Uganda and its people and in a small way sought to serve them. It was a great privilege to spend some years in that country. As my friend and colleague, Hugh Sylvester, sometime Chaplain at Budo used to say to me, "Being in Uganda is worth a guinea a minute" and he was right. Things have moved on since then, and a book such as this may not be received well in 2014. It tells of the arrival of alien influences, and that will always provoke controversy. Change is not always beneficial any more than is a resolute maintaining of the *status quo*.[6]

It is fair comment that this account is written from a European standpoint, with just another *muzungu* blundering around

---

Karugire quotes Mbaguta writing that "the Ankole natives do not like me" and "natives will not speak when my people are near." That is correct usage by a Ugandan describing other natives, and the writer is happy to be called a native of Britain.

[6]   Karugire, *op. cit.* (1973) p. 1, begins by quoting Peter Worsley: "And in the end, whatever the political style of the colonial power, Government was one of the factors bearing on the lives of the inhabitants. Missionaries, planters, prospectors, and settlers, to one extent or another, ensured that the coming of the white man did not leave the native undisturbed. He might rarely see white men, but henceforth his life would never be the same again." *The Third World*, London (1964), p. 44.

in African affairs. Yet it is not unreasonable to attempt this when the story is as much British as it is Ugandan, and this does not render invalid the information researched, the account based upon it, or even necessarily the interpretation. The inter-action between peoples can be beneficial as well as harmful, and lead to productive co-operation and respect. These quali-ties are revealed in the multi-racial origins of Mbarara, now developed as a wholly African city worthy of its place in the modern Uganda, though it did not start as such.

Another just criticism is that the book has not been proper-ly updated since most of it was written in the 1970s, and does not take account of much that may have been written since.[7] This has been impossible to achieve by one whose close con-tacts with Uganda were abruptly severed by the extremity of the political situation when he left the country, and who inevi-tably has had to move on into pressing responsibilities in other spheres.

It is also true that the treatment of the topics is uneven. The main emphasis is on the years leading up to the founding in 1898, and the first two pioneering years in 1899 and 1900. Sometimes, especially in Chapters Seven to Ten, the account continues a little into later years to put the initial stages into greater focus.

However, the writing of history is an imperfect art. No one sees all, and the best that can be achieved is faithfully to record what is found according to such understanding as may be had.

---

[7] What little I have seen amounts to this: Byaruhanga, C., *Bishop Alfred Tucker and the Establishment of the Native Anglican Church*, Nairobi (2008); Doornbos, M. R., *Not all the King's Men: Inequality as a Po-litical Instrument in Ankole*, The Hague (1978); Doornbos, M. R., *The Ankole Kingdom Controversy: Regalia Galore Revisited,* Kampala (2001); Kagume, A. M. 'Church and Society in Ankole, Uganda' PhD. University of Bristol (1993); Kahigiriza, J. *Bridging the Gap*, Kampala (2001); Steinhart, E. I., *Conflict and Collaboration: the Kingdoms of western Uganda*, Princeton (1977); Willis, J. 'Killing Bwana' *Journal of African History,* Vol. 35, No.3, (1994) pp. 379ff. Much of this is not relevant to this study. It is a disappointment that I have not seen Maari, E. 'The Growth of the Anglican Church in Ankole c. 1899–1951', M.Phil, Council for Academic Awards, (Trinity College, Bristol, 1984). This is by a former colleague and friend.

Everyone who writes must concede that interpretations may differ about any story that is told. It is reprehensible only to withhold some of the information discovered in order to slant the record towards a particular bias.

Nevertheless, even with the best of intentions it is possible that misunderstandings may arise and affront be given. My apologies are therefore offered to those who may feel that there is offence within any of these pages.

At this point it is necessary to introduce the country of Nkore to those who are unfamiliar with it. A little over a hundred years ago this was a small independent territory lying to the west of lake Victoria, and the south-west of lake Edward in Eastern Equatorial Africa. The traditional kingdom was smaller than the Ankole District of more recent times, and early European travellers described it as being about the size of Wales.[8] The two distinct tribes occupying the land were the *Bairu* cultivators and the *Bahima* cattle people. A small group of the latter were an elite known as the *Bahinda,* from among whom the *Omugabe* (king) was chosen as absolute ruler of the whole. Nevertheless, the *Bahima* only accounted for about five per cent of the population.[9] To the immediate south, across the Kagera river (which became the border with German territory, and which is now the country of Tanzania) a kindred people occupied Karagwe, while to the west there dwelt the *Banyarwanda* (in modern Rwanda). These, as well as the *Baganda* to the north of Lake Victoria sometimes posed a violent threat.

The traditional way of life was essentially of an agrarian subsistence nature. In parts of the country European travellers came upon people living in groupings of huts, sometimes even describing them as large villages or towns. One major settlement was the capital, known as the *orurembo,* or cattle *kraal* of the king. This was an encampment of huts occupied nomadically by the *Omugabe* and his court. However, with pasturage inevitably soon exhausted, the court often moved on from one

---

[8]   Perhaps with the more accurate eye of the map-maker, Major E. M. Jack described Ankole District in about 1907 as "about three-quarters the size of Wales", *On the Congo Frontier*, London (1915), p. 14.

[9]   Macallister to Ternan, 15th July 1899, ESA A/4/19/469 No. 15.

location to another. Nowhere was there a permanent settlement which could be equated with a municipality in the modern sense.[10]

The township of Mbarara has developed around the site of the headquarters of the administration which was set up in Ankole when the British first extended their control over the territory to incorporate it into the Uganda Protectorate at the very end of the nineteenth century. Although this post was established at a place which had been occupied by the king's *orurembo* on more than one occasion in the past, there was no other continuity between the two kinds of settlement. The East Africa Royal Commission of 1955 asserted that as new areas were brought under European administration, headquarters were set up which was the origin of many of the larger towns of East Africa today. This conclusion is not entirely true,[11] though the establishment of Mbarara as the major town in Ankole does follow this pattern.

Once this alien centre had been introduced into the country, the king's court soon became permanently settled there as well. With power now firmly concentrated in this place the circumstances were ripe for other aspects of urban life to grow up here too. The arrival of traders at this route centre led to the establishment of shops; missionary activity resulted in the building of churches and schools; the growing population supporting all these activities necessitated the development of housing; and the presence of a medical doctor was soon required, so that in time a hospital became essential also. Therefore from small beginnings something altogether new in the land came into being within a few years as a recognisable

---

[10]   See also below, Chapter Ten.

[11]   *East African Royal Commission Report 1953-55,* H.M.S.O., 1955 (Cmd 9475) p. 200. Twaddle, M. 'The Founding of Mbale' *Uganda Journal* (hereafter *UJ*) 30 (1966) p. 25 makes clear that further studies on the establishment of other towns in East Africa will be needed before any conclusions can be drawn about their real origins. This book provides one such, and the case of Mbarara upholds the opinion of the Commission so that Mbale may be an exception; see also Weekes, D. 'John Macallister and the Town of Mbarara 1898–1900' *UJ* 37 (1973) p. 48 note 3.

modern township. With the name Mbarara, this place has continued to develop as the capital of the district. I read that it is now a city with a population approaching a hundred thousand

However, this is to anticipate, for all this change is discussed more fully in Chapter Ten. Moreover, there was an essential prerequisite before such development could even begin. It was necessary for the *Banyankore* to enter into some kind of positive engagement with Europeans in general, and after 1890 it was with the British in particular that they had to treat.

CHAPTER TWO

THE FIRST EUROPEAN TRAVELLERS IN NKORE

When the writer lived in Mbarara the town was thought to contain some 16,000 inhabitants (1970). Over the forty years since
then it has grown to more than five times that size, and is now
listed as the eighth largest city of Uganda.[12] The account which
follows maintains that this place has its origins as a municipality in multi-racial collaboration a little over a hundred years
ago. Though this is generally accepted, it needs to be explained
how this endeavour by Africans, Asians and Europeans came
about. Though there had been Arab traders in the region for
some time previous to the first coming of Europeans, they had
no direct hand in the foundation of this modern settlement.

Any understanding of this interaction between races must
begin with the fact that in the interlacustrine region of East Africa there was inhibition about two rulers meeting face to face.
This seems to have been for a variety of reasons. Such an encounter was thought to lead to misfortune or death. When the
first European visitors came to Nkore they were regarded by
the inhabitants as returning *Bacwezi*, the pale skinned and
semi-mythical ruling dynasty whose members had suddenly
vanished some five hundred years before.[13] Suicide might even

---

[12]   In 2011 the Uganda Bureau of Statistics estimated the Mbarara
        population at 82,000.

[13]   Katate, A. G. and Kamugungunu, L., *Abagabe b'Ankole,* Dar-es-
        Salaam, (1956) Book 2, p. 61. I am grateful to Mr Edward Kanyesigye
        for translations. Such were the views of the earlier writers, though
        doubted by more recent ones. Thus Karugire simply allows that Ntare
        would not meet Cunningham because he "judged it not yet safe" and
        admits that he never did, *op. cit.* (1971) p. 246. Kagume only says that
        "it is not clear why" unless he feared their power to take away his
        own. *op. cit.* p. 33.

be preferred to unwelcome contact in which one must acknowledge the other as superior.[14]

Although a meeting between the *Omugabe* and a European was thus prevented by custom, contact was still possible. Among the *Banyankore* there was fortunately a means by which the *Omugabe* could avoid meeting a stranger and yet hospitality (*obufura*) could be extended to such visitors. This was provided by the traditional ceremony signifying friendship which was called *omukago* (blood-brotherhood), for it could be carried out through an intermediary. This barrier would some-how have to be overcome before there could be any real col-

H. M. STANLEY, the first European to become a blood-brother of the *Bahinda* rulers of Nkore

laboration between the two races. Therefore as essential background to chronicling the founding of Mbarara it is helpful to record the early contacts between Europeans and the *Omugabe* Ntare V, who ruled Nkore for about two decades until his death in 1895. All these necessarily had to be conducted through envoys acting as intermediaries.

Stanley was the first white man known to have entered the country. British born. Henry Morton Stanley, whose rise to fame began in the U.S.A., came with Francis Pocock,

---

[14]　That the earlier writers should be trusted is demonstrated by the undoubted suicide of Musinga. Kagume tells us that Racey's men "forced Musinga, king of Igara, to commit suicide." *op. cit.* p. 54. That is one way of putting it, but it can be misleading. It conjures up visions of him being forced to drink hemlock at gunpoint, or having some other brutal fate inflicted on him. Morris has a more accurate account: "In January 1901 an attempt was made to bring Musinga, the *Omukama* of Igara, into Mbarara to acknowledge Kahaya as his ruler. Musinga agreed to make the journey but custom decreed that *Abakama* should never meet one another. Furthermore, Musinga feared that he would suffer the same fate [banishment] as his enemy Igumira. On reaching the Kandekye, which was the boundary of his kingdom, Musinga produced a hidden knife and disembowelled himself." *op. cit.* (1962) p. 36. This was not at all anticipated by Racey.

the son of a Kentish fisherman. Together they passed briefly through the very north of the country in January 1876 looking for Lake "Muta Nzige."[15] At this time two princely claimants, Mukwenda and Ntare, were still disputing over the succession to the "throne" of Nkore, after the death of the *Omugabe* Mutambuka.[16] In any case the travellers made no attempt to contact the leaders of Nkore, and their presence seems to have passed unnoticed. No other Europeans are known to have entered the country before Stanley returned more than thirteen years later in July 1889, this time with Emin Pasha.[17]

Before the death of Ntare in July 1895 there were four certain occasions on which the rite of *omukago* (and/or treaties) were entered into with a European.[18] The first of these involved members of the Emin Pasha Relief Expedition. On the march this represented a considerable army quite well armed. Moreover the news had spread to Ntare that this force had several times defeated bands of men under Kabarega, the ruler of Bunyoro. Under such circumstances it is hardly surprising that

---

[15]   Lake *Muta Nzige* in *Luganda* means "it kills locusts" and it has been applied to several lakes in Uganda, including what are now Lakes George and Edward. When Stanley was in Buganda in 1875–76 he asked to be guided to *Muta Nzige* and was led to Lake George, but Lakes George and Edward were for some years not clearly distinguished, and the name was at times attached to the latter, Thomas, H. B. and Dale, I. R., 'Uganda Place Names: Some European Eponyms', *UJ* 17/2 (1953) p. 106. However, Baker's *Muta Nzige* was Lake Albert. Macallister's Map of 1900 shows "L. Albert Edward *(Lwitanzige)* (Kazinga)" and Lake George is described simply as "L. Dweru". Dr S. R. Karugire gives "L. Rweni" (Edward) and "L. Masyoro" (George), *A history of the Kingdom of Nkore in Western Uganda to 1896*, Oxford (1971), pp. 274–275.

[16]   For the last expedition by Mutesa of Buganda to aid Mukwenda between August 1876 and June 1877, Gray, Sir John, 'A history of Ankole', p. 44 note, unpublished copy in possession of Royal Commonwealth Society, Library, and quoted with the kind permission of the Librarian and Mr, A. T. Matson, the literary executor, who has also deposited a copy in the Uganda Society library.

[17]   Together with other Europeans – see the following note.

[18]   A list of all the Europeans who visited Nkore in the twenty-five years up to the signing of the Ankole Agreement in 1901 appears in Appendix A.

the weird strangers and their party were much feared. Dr
Karugire tells us that

> The full impact of this new element – the European – was
> neither felt nor understood. ... Suffice it to say that their
> presence, though a source of public amazement and curiosi-
> ty, was viewed by many with great disquiet, for no one
> knew why they had suddenly appeared, almost from no-
> where. ... [This] could not have failed to cause uneasiness
> among a population in which the incomprehensible was al-
> ways equated with the supernatural.[19]

Ntare made sure that Stanley's messengers were told that he
was away on a raiding expedition and took great care to avoid
a meeting, but later determined to secure Stanley's pacific intentions by inviting him to make *omukago*.

'NTALI'S GIFT TO STANLEY'

---

[19]   Karugire, *op. cit.* (1971) p. 246. As for Kabarega of Bunyoro, matters
of history always have more than one side to them. He was a
traditional ruler who hoped to revive flagging fortunes through trading
in slaves and ivory. Then, as now, such activities may be condemned
yet, no doubt for other reason, he was declared a national hero in
Uganda in 2009.

For this ceremony, Bucunku, the *Omugabe's* cousin was sent to act as proxy:

> He was a sweet-faced, gentle boy of about thirteen or fourteen years old, a true Mhuma with Abyssinian features. He was accompanied by his governor, or guardian, an officer in command of the spearmen and carbine-armed guards of the Prince. He gave us two large steers. ...[20]

Stanley goes on to describe in detail what occurred.

> On the 23rd [July 1889] the ceremony passed off with considerable éclat. The Zanzibaris, Soudanese, and Manyuemas were all under arms ready to salute the Prince. ... The Maxim was also in order to assist with its automatic action. The rite of blood-brotherhood began with the laying of a Persian carpet, upon which the Prince and I took our seats cross-legged, with the left hands clasped across the knees. The Professors of the Art advanced, and made an incision in each left arm, and ... took a small portion of butter, and two leaflets which served as platters, mixed it with our blood, and then exchanging the leaves, our foreheads were rubbed with the mixture. The ceremony was thus relieved of the repulsiveness which accompanies it when performed among the Congo tribes.

What happened thereafter is described in kindly terms by the explorer:

> Then the Prince, who was now my young brother, took me by the hand into my hut to smile and look pleased ... [thereafter gifts were given] the Rifles then fired five rounds each, to the boy's great admiration, but the showers of the Maxim and the cloud of dust raised by the bullets on the face of the opposite hill simply sent him into ecstasies, and ... he laid his hand firmly over his mouth.

Among the travellers there were different opinions about this, one being that he feared his teeth might snap through excessive "chattering in terror" but Stanley "firmly maintained that it was from childlike wonder and pleasure." Though there is no other hint of it in his account, it is said that he had refused to go through with the full traditional ceremony of *omukago*, so that no blood was drunk. However, whether there is any truth

---

[20]   Stanley, H. M., *op. cit.* (1890), Vol. II p.348–349 for this and the following quotes. He also met Christian exiles, p.350–352.

in this it seems to have been accepted as a genuine act.[21]

At the end of 1890 Emin, who was now representing German East Africa, contacted Ntare from Bukoba. He passed northwards through Nkore in April 1891, followed shortly by Stuhlmann who was really of his party. Unaware of the incomprehensible and totally artificial arrangement made in Berlin in July 1890 that the British and German spheres to the west of Lake Victoria should be divided by a line drawn along the first parallel of latitude south, Ntare sent envoys to Bukoba to make an alliance with the Germans, in the same month that Emin returned through his territory.[22] This approach was natural enough since Stanley had disappeared across the border into Karagwe (in the German sphere), and some time later Emin had contacted Ntare from that direction. The *Omugabe* was really seeking allies to help him against his enemies. He had already asked Emin to assist him, but without success, and it must have been particularly baffling now to be informed by Langheld, the German official at Bukoba, that no alliance could be made because Nkore lay in the British sphere.[23]

---

[21]   In discussing this Lukyn Williams is clear that the *Banyankore* did not regard Stanley's ceremony as a binding ceremony, 'Blood Brotherhood in Ankole' *UJ* 2/5 (1935), p.40. However, the evidence produced by Doornbos, and the letter which Bucunku wrote to Stanley in Oct. 1902 (which he quotes) seem to indicate beyond a doubt that Bucunku, sand the *Banyankore* did regard it as binding during the lifetime of the two participants, though this fact may have been forgotten or denied later; 'Stanley's Blood Brotherhood' *UJ* 30/2 (1966) pp. 209–210. For more about Apolo Bucunku, see note 184.

There may be those interested in the fact that *omukago* is broken by death. Stanley died on 10th May 1904; thousands of miles away Bucunku succumbed to smallpox in the following month.

[22]   See Gray, *op. cit.* (1952), pp. 52–53.

[23]   Imperialists could be aware of the absurdity of some of the actions they had to take. Major E. M. Jack, of the Royal Engineers, (see note 8 above) will be quoted later in describing Mbarara (1907), of which he was clearly fond. He explains how he came to be in East Africa, *op. cit.,* pp. 17–18. "Some years ago ... certain diplomatists said that the boundary between the British and Belgian territory in Central Africa – to wit, the Uganda Protectorate and the Congolese Free State (as it was then called) – should be the 30th Meridian east of Greenwich. That no one knew with absolute certainty where the 30th Meridian was did not

That Ntare had already sought to make an alliance with the Germans is an important fact to remember when considering Lugard's activities in Nkore in the months immediately following. As a result of preliminary contacts with Ntare, Zakariah Kizito (a young *Muganda* Christian refugee who later returned home and became prominent in his own country) was sent ahead to explain Lugard's intentions. At the end of June he met Lugard at Nyabuszhozi, bringing him a relation of Ntare's called Bireri. On 1st July Bireri and Lugard went through a fully traditional ceremony of *omukago,* and at the same time a treaty was signed to the effect that Nkore was placed under the suzerainty of the Imperial British East Africa Company (hereafter IBEACo).

Both Ntare and Lugard were seeking to make an alliance, and one was made, though it is not at all clear exactly what each meant by it, nor did it come to mean a great deal in practice. Once again the act of *omukago* seems to have been accepted as genuine;[24] De Winton followed Lugard through

---

deter the frontier-makers; agreements were made, and a straight line was drawn on a map of pleasing appearance. Time passed on; knowledge advanced by slow degrees; and eventually it was found that the 30th Meridian was not where it was thought to have been. Something had moved – either the little straight line, or the lakes and rivers so delightfully portrayed. It did not matter whichever, but it did rather matter how these lakes and mountains were situated with regard to the little straight line. Each side, oddly enough, took the view which gave to them the larger amount of territory. ..." Thus the need for an accurate map – which Jack and his colleagues surveyed. He went on to become a distinguished cartographer and Director-General of the Ordnance Survey in Britain 1922–1930. See also note 42.

[24]   This is discussed by Lukyn Williams, *op. cit.* 2/5 (1935) pp. 205–8; Morris prints the treaty in *A History of Ankole,* Nairobi (1962), pp. 46–47. The identity of the person with whom Lugard made *omukago* is a little obscure. Lugard called him Birinzi, and he is usually identified with Bireri (Birere) whom Lukyn Williams calls Ntare's uncle. Locally, however, there is some uncertainty: "This Prince Birere (Birenzi) is regarded by some as Ruhiigwa, grandfather of Princess Kajangire; others say that Teofilo Rwamukwaya also befriended the European, but it is not known which. But others insist that Birere was still alive, since the Muti smallpox had not occurred. It is this smallpox which killed Birere at Nyabiherere, Kikyenkye, near Rwomuhoro." Katate and Kamugungunu, *op. cit,* Bk. 2, pp. 76–77. In view of the last

Ankole and was well received, as was the latter on his return. Lugard was never in a position to follow up the treaty.[25]

The next encounter with Europeans was a most unhappy affair. In July 1893 Langheld obtained verbal permission in Kampala to pass through the British sphere if necessary on a visit to German Rwanda. In the event difficulties were encountered in Mpororo and he decided to call on the British officer at Fort George. Making his way to Katwe he found the fort abandoned, and so decided to return the quickest way, i.e. through Nkore. Failing to understand the local custom which made the *Omugabe* unwilling to meet with a European, Langheld inadvertently insisted on taking a route which passed very close to Ntare's capital. This provoked a show of force by the *Banyankore* on the 12th September, when trouble was averted by Langheld on the one side and the leading chiefs on the other. The following day Langheld moved on to Birere, a few miles south of the Muti hills, but a clash did occur there when "at least twenty *Banyankole* were killed including ten of their leading men." Langheld made for Bukoba as quickly as possible. He was followed into Karagwe by messengers from Ntare who made it clear that the *Omugabe* had not been responsible for the trouble, and reiterated his wish to make an alliance with the Germans. Langheld again had to decline, but when asked to send Ntare a coffee bean soaked in his blood for the purposes of making *omukago,* he agreed. Not long after that the envoy, a *Mwiru* called Ishingoma, returned with a present of ivory and another blood stained bean.[26]

Confirmation that this rather rudimentary ceremony was accepted by the *Banyankore* seems to come from the treatment accorded to the Scottish naturalist, Scott Elliot, who crossed

---

comment identification with Birere seems most likely.

[25] Dr Karugire has fairly shown that it was absurd for an official of the Company to pledge protection to Ntare "since its officials – or what remained of them – in East Africa did not have adequate protection for themselves." *op. cit.* (1971) p. 246.

[26] For Langheld's expedition see, Gray *op. cit.* (1952) pp. 58–60. The account there is based on Langheld's own record in Langheld, W. *Zwanzig Jahre in Deutschen Kolonnien*, Berlin (1909).

from German territory in March 1894. Having previously sent some men under an *askari,* Taritibu, "with an old tweed suit and sundries to Antari. He ... made Antari believe I was a most important personage." Ntare responded by sending "a big chief Lukala" to act as guide, and the traveller certainly experience no difficulties.

Nevertheless the *Omugabe* now seemed to realise that he must look elsewhere than to the Germans for allies. Apparently troubled by raids from the *Banyarwanda,* he sent an appeal for help to the British at Entebbe in the middle of 1894. This request reached Colvile[27] at the same time as the news that J. P. Wilson, *en route* for Toro, was pinned down in Kabula by the *Futabangi* (*Bhang*-smoking *Baganda*).[28] There was also the need to stop illicit arms passing through to Kabarega in Bunyoro, so it proved convenient to send Major G. G. Cunningham to escort Wilson to his place of work and to visit Nkore. All these journeys and contacts are discussed more fully in Appendix A.[29] Moreover, it is interesting to record the details of Cunningham's journey through Nkore in 1894 because it has previously been somewhat misunderstood. This is done in the Appendix C. He also provided a map and much greater knowledge of Ntare's country than had previously been available to Europeans.

---

[27]   In the first decade the chief British Government official in Uganda was designated 'Commissioner, Commander-in-Chief and Consul-General.' The term Governor was used from 1905–1962.

[28]   Colvile, H. E. *Land of the Nile Springs,* London, (1895), pp. 287–290. Colvile quotes the letter he received (as Commissioner) from J. P. Wilson, dated Marongo, 17th July 1894, ESA file 4/2/2. *Futabangi* were *Bhang*-smokers among the *Baganda. Bhang* is cannabis. This has a long history of infusion in India.

[29]   There is a fuller discussion in Weekes, D. *Ankole Religion and Christianity* (forthcoming).

CHAPTER THREE

THE *OMUGABE* FIRST MEETS A EUROPEAN

It may seem surprising that the origins of Mbarara as a permanent settlement are to be found in the coming of European administration. This was extended to include Nkore (anglicised as Ankole) in 1896, although it did not begin to become effective until 1898.[30] The establishment of the civil station at Mbarara dates from this time, though we should note how the station site had been occupied prior to this.

Two local historians record that "When the *Omugabe* Ntare V left Kaigoshora, a place of rinderpest, he settled at Muti (present Mbarara Township)".[31] Ntare was living here at the time when Lugard passed through to the north in June 1891.[32] It was here that the dreaded Omuze Gwa Muti (the Muti smallpox) broke out, which killed so many of the leading people, including Ntare's son Kabumbire. However, this place of unhappy memories was abandoned, and Ntare later occupied a site across the river at Katete. He also lived for a time at Kaburangire (about four miles towards Masaka) and at a site adjacent to the Muti one called after the grass, Mburara.

Lugard was concerned with Ankole because of his desire to prevent arms and ammunition coming into Buganda by this route and to promote trade "by means of a treaty with Ntali to this end, and by establishing, if possible stations in his coun-

---

[30] *Ibid* where this is fully discussed, especially Chapters 3 & 5 (some of which is included here in this Chapter).

[31] Katate and Kamugungunu, *op. cit.* Bk. 1, p. 143.

[32] Perham, M. *The Diaries of Lord Lugard,* London, (1959), Vol. 2, p. 225. Lukyn Williams, F., in 'Early travellers in Ankole' *UJ* **2/3**, 1935, p. 206 says that Ntare was living near Kakiika, three miles north of Mbarara, but such a site at Kakiika is not now remembered, and Muti would seem to be much more likely.

try."[33] The first of these objectives was achieved by the treaty and blood-brotherhood *(omukago)* made in Nyabushozi but

> I had abandoned the idea of building a station in Ankole, at least for the present, for there was no food for a garrison. Moreover the station would naturally be built at the capital; and as this proved to be so far south and out of my route, I decided not to visit it now.[34]

Then in 1893 two significant things happened. The first is described by Scott Elliot:

> A German expedition, under Captain Langheld, had, for purposes which I do not understand, passed through Ankole a short time before my arrival (March 1894), The leader wished, contrary to the expressed desire of Antari, to proceed to the latter's capital, and was in consequence attacked."[35]

As a result of this Ntare appealed for the protection promised in Lugard's treaty.[36] The second was Sir Gerald Portal's mission to Uganda, the report of which was published in March 1894. As a result the decision was taken which led to the declaration of the Uganda Protectorate over the Kingdom of Buganda.

The arrangements in the adjoining areas of "Koki, Ankole, Bunyoro and Busoga" were to

> be limited to the agreements with the Chiefs which may be required for maintaining friendly relations and alliance between them and the Protectorate for securing facilities for trade and for suppressing the slave-trade.[37]

This last motive for the creation of the Protectorate is often overlooked. The problem has been discussed in Chapter One, but eradication remained incomplete as long as slaves could be taken out of Central Africa by routes where Britain could not seal off the coasts. The Brussels Act (1890) had authorized in-

---

[33] Lugard, F. J. D., *The Rise of our East African Empire,* Edinburgh (1893), Vol. 2, p. 136, see above note 25.

[34] *Ibid,* p. 160.

[35] Elliot, G. F. Scott, A *Naturalist in Mid-Africa,* London (1896), p. 76.

[36] Morris, H. F., *op. cit.,* p. 16, see above note 27.

[37] Quoted in Hill, M. F., *Permanent Way,* Nairobi (1949), Vol. 1, p. 125.

ternational action to suppress the trade in the interior.[38] Any doubt that this objective was high on the British agenda in coming to Uganda should be removed by the number of references to it in the official correspondence. They are convincing evidence, and some are quoted within these pages. By way of example, one can look at the statements made in 1896 by the Commissioner, and by a missionary in Koki, both specific about the need to end the slave trade.[39]

In order to carry out instructions Colonel Colvile, who had arrived in Buganda in November 1893, proclaimed the Protectorate at Mengo on 27th August 1894. Two days later a new treaty with Ntare was concluded by Major G. G. Cunningham (Derby Regiment).

Colville sent Cunningham to Nkore because he believed "that a considerable trade in arms and ammunition passed through Ankole on its way to Kabarega" and thus "was anxious to place a small post there to stop it."[40] At the same time he did not wish to alienate Ntare and no garrison was to be left there without his full consent. As it turned out this was not forthcoming and no post was established, but in his report Cunningham gave his opinion that "with regard to a post to stop illicit trade, I think it should be at Ntali's."[41] In fact the new treaty achieved little more than had Lugard.

These treaties have been described as "the smartest confidence trick that all empire builders used in this region. It was a trick, because it is not clear that the rulers had any idea of what these treaties were all about."[42] Leaving aside the extraordinary

---

[38]   These matters, and the controversy in Britain against creating the Protectorate, are discussed in works like, Perham, M. *Lugard The Years of Adventure 1858–98,* London (1956).

[39]   See note 46 and note n. in Appendix A below.

[40]   Colvile, H. E. *op. cit.,* p. 290.

[41]   G. G. Cunningham to H. E. Colvile 24th September 1894 Entebbe Secretariat Archives (hereafter ESA) A/2/3.

[42]   Karugire, S. R., *op. cit.* (1971) p 246. This otherwise apparently admirable work is marred when the colonial period is discussed. Dr. Karugire insists on bringing the politics of the post-independence period into discussion of the 1890s, and thereby loses his credibility. Criticism of such treaties existed in Britain fully two decades earlier,

claim that Stanley was given Nkore by Ntare, the fairness of such criticisms can be challenged. Certainly Ntare was sufficiently aware of the contents of his dealings with Lugard to remember them when Germans entered his territory, as we have just observed, and Cunningham's treaty was to lead to an appeal to the Protectorate Government after Ntare's death.

Such treaties were part of the paraphernalia of the encounter between the *Banyankore* and the British in which both sides were equally ignorant of the language and customs of the other. By Dr Karugire's definition both the ceremonies of blood-brotherhood into which Stanley and Lugard were pressed, and the later offer of marriage made to influence Macallister,[43] were just as much 'tricks'. The Europeans involved clearly did not properly understand what these rites signified, any more than Kahitsi did in offering a bride to the Sub-Commissioner, but to use the emotive word 'trick' is to miss the point entirely. The truth is that the two sides were poles apart, and while the *Banyankore* made alliances by marriage and by blood-brotherhood (as Dr. Karugire ably demonstrates), the British made alliances by printed treaty. Neither side fully understood the other in these things, but that does not mean that there was a deliberate deception. The basic fact is that the treaties and the blood-brotherhoods were the first steps in building a bridge between the two cultures. The surprising thing is not that they failed to understand each other fully, but that they understood each other at all.

Cunningham's treaty made on the standard printed 'Treaty Form' of the time, stated

that British subjects shall have free access to all parts of

---

for their uncertain status was thoroughly appreciated, and lampooned in Sir W. S. Gilbert's satire, "The three kings of Chickeraboo' printed in *The Bab Ballads*, London (1873).

The admiral pleased with his welcome warm,
Unrolled a printed Alliance form.
'Your majesty sign me this, I pray –
I come in a friendly kind of way –
I come, if you please, with the best intents,
And Queen Victoria's compliments'.

[43]   See below footnote 139.

> Ankole, and shall have the right to build houses and possess
> property according to the laws in force in this country; that
> they shall have full liberty to carry on such trade or manu-
> facture as may be approved by Her Majesty. ...[44]

Such provisions do not seem to have reflected very accurately
the actual state of affairs. One part of the country to which
British subjects certainly did not have access was anywhere
that Ntare himself might be found. Despite attempts to lead
him in the wrong direction. Cunningham managed to get within "sight of Ntali's town," only to find that the king had fled to
the hills and "was decidedly averse to the establishment of a
post in his country." Certainly nothing was done by the British
to implement the treaty.[45]

Ntare died in July 1895 and in the ensuing rivalry for power between two of the leading princes *(Bahinda),* Kahisti and
Igumira, appeal was made to the Protectorate Government and
to the *Kabaka* of Buganda on behalf of each candidate. The
difficulty of securing stability in areas such as Ankole, which
were within the British sphere but not included in the Protectorate, led to this being extended in July 1896. However, just
as the I.B.E.A. Company had not been in a position to assert
itself in Nkore, neither was the new administration. Short of
both men and resources, the Commissioner was unable to
spare anyone to set up a new station, though he considered this
to be very necessary "both for the proper supervision of the
province itself, and for the contraband trade in powder and
caps, and the slave-raiding which, it cannot well be doubted,
still continues over the German frontier."[46] Missionaries were
also concerned, but unable to act.

Finally when the British penetrated into Nkore, it was a
case of 'needs must'. The *Kabaka* Mwanga fled from Mengo
secretly on 5th July 1897, and headed west. Ternan, the Acting

---

[44] Quoted in Morris, *op. cit.* (1962) p. 47.

[45] Colvile, *op. cit.,* pp. 292–294. The use of the word 'town' here is
subject to the limitations already described. It was almost entirely
pastoral, and was not permanent.

[46] E. J. L. Berkeley (Commissioner) to F. O. 19th November 1896, ESA
A/34/2/123.

Commissioner, mustered the available men and sent them to Buddu. William Grant, in charge there, was given this instruction:

> though the present operations are not in any way conducted for the purpose of the conquest of Ankole, you need have no hesitation in entering that country if your operations should require it, particularly if you are assured that it is affording help to the rebels.[47]

It was not known what the attitude of the rulers of Nkore would be and accordingly messengers were first sent. Kahaya was nominally the *Omugabe* but power lay in the hands of the Regents, Igumira and Kahitsi, who had asked for outside support in 1895. It seems that Kahitsi and Kahaya were against helping the rebels, while Igumira was responsible for the contingent from Nkore, led by "Vagooto (Mbaguta), the King of Ankole's Mujasi," who had been fighting with the forces under Gabrieli Kintu.[48]

'CHIEF IGUMIRA IN HIS "KITWARRARRI"'

---

[47]   G. Wilson to W. Grant, 28 August 1897, ESA A/5/3/255.

[48]   *Papers Relating to the Events in the Uganda Protectorate,* London, H.M.S.O. 1898, C. 8941 (Africa no. 2); G. Wilson to the Marquess of Salisbury, No. 16, 15th September 1898, p. 14 and W. Grant to G. Wilson, 23th August 1897, p. 16.

George Wilson, the Acting Commissioner, added in his report to the Marquess of Salisbury that,

> mainly with a view to precipitating a change of policy on the part of Ankole, I have also menaced that country with two armed forces, on its north-eastern and north-western frontiers, under Captain Sitwell and Mr. Malek respectively.[49]

Whether this was the deciding factor, or not, Kahaya's answer was again favourable to European intervention; Grant wrote to Wilson that

> it appears that Kahaya is most anxious that the rebels, including the *Wangoni*, should be driven out of his country, but he thinks himself not sufficiently powerful to do the work alone. He is willing (from all accounts) to give me all the assistance in his power, and is ready to point out where the rebels are hiding.[50]

During September 1897 Grant conducted a chase after Kintu but failed to repeat the victory he had had over the rebels at Nyendo hill, near Masaka on 23th August. After that experience the rebels avoided a pitched battle, and largely managed to keep one step ahead of Grant, even after he had divided his forces. Lieutenant Hobart's column in particular did a lot of travelling in the eastern part of Ankole. By the end of the month Grant was able to report to Wilson: "Came to the conclusion that it was useless following them up as it might mean months of marching and counter marching;" and added optimistically: "I feel inclined to think that the rebels have had a severe punishment and that the few who are now with Gabriel (Kintu) are only waiting for the opportunity to desert him."[51]

---

[49]   *Ibid.* Wilson to Salisbury, p. 15.

[50]   W. Grant to G. Wilson, 15th September 1897, ESA. A/4/9/396. The Revd H. Clayton, C.M.S., writing from Koki, 11th July 1897, described the Wangoni as "a set of *Baganda* called the *bhang* (Indian hemp) smokers, who at present live on the borders of Ankole. These are some of the most determined old heathen who found a refuge in Ankole, and they are known to be most bitter against all Europeans and readers of any kind," see above note 28.

[51]   Grant to Wilson, 30th September 1897, ESA A/4/9/416. In his report to Salisbury (reprinted in Africa no. 2 (1898) *op. cit.,* p. 14) Wilson describes receiving news of the action at Nyendo on 28th August, but

It was these events which led to a curious report reaching Captain Sitwell, the officer-in-charge in Toro. In his diary for the 26th September 1897 he writes: "Kagero says it is true that Katabarwa is dead, that a European is in Ankole, that he has built a *boma* on the Ruwezi River near Ntali's."[52] This sounds as though it records the earliest European settlement at what is now Mbarara. In fact a careful examination of the evidence shows that all the information Kagero gave was incorrect, though founded on some fact. Katabarwa was amongst the wounded at Nyendo Hill, but he certainly did not die of these wounds.[53] Hobart reported to Grant that on 12th September he

> camped for the night on the shore of lake Villiers called by the natives Kachera. On the 13th the north end of the lake.
> … On the 14th we moved down the east shore of the lake
> … learned that Katabulua and the principal rebel leaders who were with him had already effected their escape into German territory.[54]

It was this activity which presumably gave rise to Kagero's report.

Hobart continued in the area of east Ankole but by the end of September the Acting Commissioner had his hands full in another direction. The Sudanese Mutiny had broken out in Buganda, and once again it became impossible to think seriously of setting up an administration in a new area.

Attention was once more centred on Nkore at the end of the year when Mwanga escaped from German territory and was reported to be in that area with a large number of guns. Sitwell received orders to cut off Mwanga's route to the north by holding the Bwera-Lwenkula frontier, but later moved down into Ankole where he narrowly missed Kintu in March. A month later (April 1898) he missed him again at Ruaboyo, at

---

does not give the actual date. This probably gave rise to the error on the metal plate affixed to the memorial cairn at Masaka fort where the date of the action is wrongly given as the 28th.

[52] Captain C. G. H. Sitwell, 'Diary' in ESA, 26th September 1897.

[53] Wright, M. *The Baganda in the Heroic Age,* Nairobi, (1971) p. 193.

[54] Lt. C. V. C. Hobart to Grant, 29th September 1897, ESA A/4/9/9 with 416.

which point he was recalled to Lwenkula.[55]

Kintu continued to give trouble and in the middle of 1898 Captain M. J. Tighe was sent to Masaka with Hobart under him. It was reported that Kintu was planning an evasive withdrawal into Nkore, with the object of enticing the punitive expedition after him and then doubling back to devastate the defenceless Buddu Province.

The attitude of Kahaya, the young ruler of Nkore, was doubtful, so an ultimatum was dispatched allowing him twenty days to confirm his loyalty, failing which Nkore would be declared hostile territory. Kahaya's answer reached Kabula in September, promising co-operation and hoping that a post would be maintained permanently at Kabula and another in Nkore.[56] Wilson informed the Commissioner that

> Ankole responded to the ultimatum sent by me in August by immediately detailing a useful local force to assist Captain Tighe, and its rulers have proved, throughout, their readiness to come under the protection of the Administration. Captain Tighe has reported the practical termination of the Buddu-Ankole active operations.[57]

Tighe's military operations were successful, at least as far as Nkore was concerned, and Ternan was able to report to the Commissioner in January 1899 that while he was "commanding in Ankole he effectually cleared the country of rebels."[58] Thus the way was at last prepared for the setting up of an administrative post.

However it was not just military operations that had been necessary. Afterwards Tighe claimed an allowance for the time when he "assumed political control (more particularly in connection with the King of Ankole)" and gave the dates as 27th August to 16th October. Meanwhile Berkeley had become convinced that

---

[55]   Sitwell, *op. cit.,* 10th January and 10th–12th April 1898.

[56]   Moyse-Bartlett, *op. cit.,* pp.78–79 (cf. Wilson to Berkeley, 4th September 1898, ESA A/4/12/617). Lt. General Sir Michael Tighe (1864-1925) later returned to East Africa as a Divisional Commander during the campaign 1915–16.

[57]   Wilson to Commissioner, 17th October 1898, ESA A/4/13/720.

[58]   Ternan to Commissioner, 24th January 1899, ESA A/4/15/32.

the situation in the southwestern corner of this Protectorate makes it practically imperative that administrative charge of Ankole should be taken in hand without delay. This has long been a project but has had to be continually set aside for want of officials and troops.

Advised by the O.C. Troops that a company would shortly be available, Berkeley decided to make the necessary officials available. He had planned to send Macallister (First Class Assistant) to resume the civil charge of Unyoro, but now felt himself forced by a situation which "was becoming nothing less than intolerable" to "arrange that Mr. Macallister will proceed to Antali's with an assistant and the company in question, there to take charge of the district of Ankole."[59] Though there is nothing in the official correspondence, it might seem that Macallister may have visited Nkore while Tighe was in charge there, or even earlier, and then returned to Entebbe to make the necessary preparations. This is asserted in local discussions of these events and is compounded because in a private letter to Stanley Tomkins dated 6th May 1898 from Port Victoria where he was on a brief visit Macallister wrote "leave here to go to Ankole." [60]

At the end of September he still had not been able to go. When Berkeley left on a tour of the eastern districts, he informed the Foreign Office from Mumias that "Mr. Macallister was about to leave Kampala to take up his duties in that district (Ankole) the chiefs and people of which appear to have made up their minds to side with the Administration."[61]

---

59   Tighe to Adjutant, 27th Baluchi Light Infantry, 4th January 1899, ESA A/4/15/2. Berkeley to OC troops, 13th August 1898, ESA A/5/4/186 and Berkeley to Major Martyr, 24th August 1898, ESA A/5/4/209.

60   Katate and Kamugungunu, *op. cit.,* Bk. 2, pp. 4–5; *Ebigano by'ebyabaireho Omuri Uganda,* edited by H. W. R. Hawes, book 2, p. 42; Karugire, *op. cit.* (1971) p. 249. See also Macallister's letter ESA A/4/11/302-303 (between). The 1897 date for this given by Karugire and others is impossible as Macallister left Port Victoria for the coast in January 1897 and did not return from leave till February 1898. Any date earlier than 1897 would also appear unlikely as Macallister was at Port Victoria throughout 1895 and 1896.

61   Berkeley to F.O. 10th October 1898, ESA A/3/4/157.

Even so there was to be further delay, this time caused by
the unexpected rebel activity in the north in which Lieutenant
Hannyngton was badly wounded and Kizalizi fort "invested."
George Wilson, left in charge at Kampala, found it necessary
to

> recall the company of the 27th Bombay Infantry from Bud-
> du, and to despatch with Captain Fowler, the half company
> of Uganda Rifles intended for Ankole. These movements
> must of course have a detrimental effect on the position in
> Buddu and Ankole, where affairs had assumed, as I have
> previously stated, a most satisfactory aspect.[62]

Doubtless it had been intended that Macallister should take
over politically as soon as Tighe left Nkore, but in spite of the
frustration of further delay he continued to make the necessary
preparations and sent in estimates "for the district of Ankole
1899–1900" on 1st November.[63] In the end it was not until 2nd
December 1898 that his caravan was able to leave Kampala on
its way westward.[64] "The party was met at the frontier by
Mbaguta with a party of his *Abagonya.*" As Mbaguta afterwards explained, Macallister's arrival was not at all welcome
to certain sections of the community. Nevertheless the march
to Mbarara was accomplished without any untoward inci-
dent.[65]

We have seen how a meeting with the *Omugabe* and Europeans was inhibited by custom. Nevertheless Stanley on his
own behalf, Lugard and Cunningham for the British, and Emin
and Langheld for the Germans, had contact with Ntare V

---

[62]   Wilson to Commissioner, 17th October 1898, ESA A/4/13/720.

[63]   Macallister to Berkeley, 1st November 1898, ESA A/4/13/746.

[64]   Macallister to Berkeley, 1st January 1899, ESA A/4/15/20 No.2.

[65]   Among Sir John Gray's papers at the Royal Commonwealth Society
        Library there is a file of rough translations from the vernacular
        apparently taken from *Munno.* One of these "The Words of the Hon.
        Nuwa Mbaguta – 'The Katikiro'" seems to be from February 1913. It
        includes what is perhaps Mbaguta's own account of the journey:
        "Then Mr. Makalista, whom they nicknamed Kisaka (the big) arrived.
        I myself met him at Sikamaliga, in the county of Kayima, in Ankole.
        At that journey, 1 had great trouble of supplying food to his and my
        people, because food was scarcely. I had the chance of leading him in
        a good way to where he went." I have not seen the original in *Munno.*

through envoys. When he died in 1895 the British were not strong enough to settle Nkore, and Mwanga's rebellion of 1897 threw the region into turmoil. Once that conflict was over, British administration was set up at the end of 1898. Thus sometime between Ntare's determined avoidance of meeting with Cunningham in August 1894 and December 1898 the initial meeting with the *Omugabe* occurred, for the tradition forbidding it had first to be broken before this development could take place.

As we have seen this was unlikely to have been possible earlier that 1898 and the 'window' for such a meeting in that year can be narrowed to between 1st November and 1st December. Nevertheless it is provoking to find no contemporary evidence for this encounter. *Abagabe b'Ankole,* written half a century later, enshrines the oral tradition.

> In 1897 Bwana Macallister (Kishaka) came to Ankole and found Kahaya II at Rushasha. ... Ruhara and other chiefs who were looking after Kahaya were at first reluctant to show him to the European. Then Mbaguta threatened that if they did not show him to the European he would take the latter to Rwakatogoro[66] who would become *Omugabe* instead. At this Kahaya ... was shown to the European and he was officially declared to be the new *Omugabe*. Bwana Macallister said, 'I am going back to Entebbe and I hope to return and stay here permanently.'[67].

The *Omugabe* who broke with tradition was certainly Kahaya II who had recently succeeded Ntare, and the quotation identifies the European as Macallister (the first British res-

---

[66] The background to this is confirmed by Dr Karugire. It was during the interval between Macallister's reconnaissance and permanent return that Kahitsi, who was guardian to Kahaya's property, switched his support to Rwakatogoro. However, he repeats the error that this took place in 1897, Karugire, (1973) pp. 13–14, and see above note 60. Igumira and Kahitsi were nephews of Ntare, but barred from succeeding by physical imperfection, the one having only one eye and the other being left-handed. Rwakatogoro was their nephew while Kahaya was Igumira's son, *ibid*, pp. 27–28. When Kahaya died childless in 1944 he was succeeded as *Omugabe* by Rwakatogoro's son, Gasyonga.

[67] Katate & Kamugunguru, *op. cit.*, Bk. 2, pp. 80–81.

ident) and not one of the British officers who campaigned in Nkore in 1897–98, such as Hobart and Tighe. However, a date in 1897 is not possible. Macallister's movements have been clearly plotted through the official correspondence, and for most of that year he was absent on home leave (see note 60) and, anyway, the political situation in Nkore then did not allow of it.

What then can be said of the date of the first encounter between an *Omugabe* and a European? Macallister can only have first come into the country between June and November 1898. Mbarara lies approximately one hundred and sixty miles west south-west of Kampala, and the *Omugabe* was then another ten miles further on occupying the site at Rushasha. At least three weeks would therefore be required to carry out the round trip and accomplish everything needful. The official correspondence makes the period between the 1st November and the 1st December 1898 the only real possibility but gives no actual record of it taking place. Moreover such an event fits the description given by the local historians, but not their date.

However, Macallister states in the official correspondence that he set out for Ankole on the 2nd December 1898, arrived on the 18th and next day met with Kahaya.[68] As there was no apparent difficulty in effecting this meeting, the oral tradition that Macallister had made a preliminary visit some time previously in which he "was shown" the *Omugabe* is assumed and therefore entirely endorsed as a *sine qua non*. The question of when exactly this earlier visit occurred then arises, and it is discussed in some detail in Appendix B.

For our purposes we can assume that it took place during November 1898 and that almost immediately Macallister returned to establish the Administration in Ankole. However, why did Macallister considered it necessary to go down to Nkore on a preliminary visit, and return to Entebbe,[69] only to

---

[68] Macallister to Berkeley, 1st January 1899, ESA A4/15/20/24 No.2 (both quotes).

[69] It is sometimes said that he was operating from Kampala, Karugire, *op. cit.* (1973) p. 33, but the British Government headquarters were at Entebbe and Katate & Kamugungunu are right in stating that he returned to and came back from there, (see note 67) though no doubt

set out again almost at once for his new sphere of work? There
are a number of factors to be considered.

At first very little was known by the British officials about
conditions in Nkore and in particular about the *Omugabe*'s
orurembo.[70] One obvious way to test the genuineness of Kahaya's request for a British presence was to go and confront him
with a European in person.

Then for years the Nkore situation had been confused, and
although Macallister had sent in estimates, he may well have
been very doubtful about the adequacy of the arrangements
that were being made.

Thirdly, there is the local suggestion that a dispute among
the *Bahinda* (members of the ruling clan) as to whether Rwakatogoro or Kahaya should be confirmed as *Omugabe* was in
urgent need of being settled by outside intervention.[71]

Lastly, there was the precedent of Macallister's setting up
the Administration at Port Victoria. There he had had adequate
opportunity to go and survey the area and over a period obtain
official reflection on the best place for the new station. He
considered this to be at the termination of the proposed railway
rather than at Samia's boma.[72] As for Nkore, the officially
proposed site was at the rather vague location of "Ntali's", the
orurembo of the previous *Omugabe*. Macallister, being an engineer,[73] can have been expected to want to know in some detail the site on which he was going to build, and how suitable it
was going to be.

We can now briefly diverge to consider the supplementary
interest surrounding the personality of this pioneer. The 'Dic-

---

passing through Kampala on the way. In some accounts the two place-
names seem to be used inter-changeably.

[70] The site of the cattle-kraal which served as the headquarters or capital
of the *Omugabe*.

[71] Karugire, S.R. *op. cit.* (1973) p. 34.

[72] Macallister to Commissioner, Port Alice 14th February 1895: ESA
A4/1, and Macallister to Commissioner, Ntebbi 25th June 1895: ESA
A34/1.

[73] Macallister became an Associate Member of the Institute of Civil
Engineers (A.M.I.C.E) in May 1892.

tionary of East African Biography' reveals scant details about Macallister: the dates of his life, 1862–1909; his training as an engineer; his appointment to the service of the Imperial British East Africa Company in 1890, and something of his later career in the Uganda Administration, but nothing of his social background or upbringing. Some years ago I described him as an elusive character.[74]

---

[74]   Weekes, *op. cit.* (1973) p. 49 note 36.

CHAPTER FOUR

WHO WAS JOHN MACALLISTER?

Armed with Macallister's home address in London, at Heathfield, Plumstead the Greenwich Public Library was soon able
to provide Census and other material about the family living
there. Macallister's forebears were Ulstermen from Derry. His
father was Vicar of St. Nicholas, Plumstead for forty years
having been appointed to the living in 1865 by his brother who
had become Vicar of Plumstead in the previous year. Robert
John Dudley Macallister was born at Ramsgate in 1862. The
Library also provided the interesting detail that the Reverend
John M'Allister had married the only daughter, born in India,
of Sir William Coghlan, K.C.B.

Ferreting around in the reference books revealed that "Major General William Marcus Coghlan of the Royal Artillery,
sometime political agent and military commandant at Aden"
was appointed K.C.B. in 1864. Aden appears to have been his
last military command, although already a Colonel Commandant in his regiment he continued to rise in rank, becoming
Lieutenant-General in 1872 and General five years later. He
died at Ramsgate in 1885, aged 82.[75] Thus it seems that Macallister was born at the Coghlan's home and doubtless much influenced by them.

This background becomes increasingly relevant when we
realise that Coghlan was commandant at Aden from 1854–63,
throughout the period in which Burton, Speke and Grant made
their Red Sea and East African expeditions, Indeed, Burton
wrote in 1856 of his recent sojourn in "Aden, with its dull rou-

---

[75] Boase, F. *Modern English Biography,* Truro (1892) Vol. 1, p. 663;
Army Lists; The Times, 27th November, 1885, p. 7. Shaw, W.A. *The
Knights of England,* London (1906), Vol. 1, p. 283.

tine of meaningless parades and tiresome courts martial, where society is broken by ridiculous distinctions of staff men, and regimental men, Madras men and Bombay men."[76]

Coghlan had been one of the latter, having joined the Bombay Artillery in 1820. This was the year of the birth of Arnold Burrowes Kemball who would later become a Director of the I.B.E.A.Co. and the two men later served together in the first Afghan war, eventually becoming fellow Colonels Commandant in the Royal Artillery, Generals in the Army and K.C.B. Thus Macallister, who was well into his twenties when Sir William died, was doubtless reared on tales of the East, the exploits of Burton, and of Kemball who continued in the Gulf until 1878. Kemball must have been aware that Macallister was Coghlan's grandson when he signed his contract with the I.B.E.A. Company in June 1890, becoming Executive Engineer.[77]

The *Alumni Oxonienses* includes William Marcus Coghlan McAllister named after his grandfather but entering The Queen's College, Oxford in 1879 to follow his father in the Church.[78] We have seen him as a long-time country rector in Norfolk and this led to contact with The Reverend B. R. McAllister (1903-78), John Macallister's only son (curiously succeeding generations spelt the surname slightly differently.) Unfortunately he was not able to give much more information, having been less than two when his father was last in Britain and only seven when he died in distant Africa. Nevertheless, he produced photographs and copies of the I.B.E.A.Co. contract dated 5th July 1890, and the commission as Vice-Consul in Uganda. He also stated that his paternal grandfather was an "impecunious and over productive" clergyman who found the education of his thirteen children a problem. I find that his eldest son was for seven years at school at Christ's Hospital, the third was briefly at Merchant Taylors, and the youngest at Bury St. Edmund's Grammar School and Corpus Christi Col-

---

[76]   Burton, R.F. *First Footsteps in East Africa,* London (1856) pp. 39–40.

[77]   General Sir Arnold Burrowes Kemball, (1820–1908) KCB, KCIE.

[78]   Foster, J. *Alumni Oxonienses*, 1715–1886, London (1888) Vol. 3. p. 888.

lege, Cambridge. It is no surprise therefore that some of the sons "sought to make their fortunes in the newly developing colonies": Ronald "was in Nigeria ... Adair a tea planter in India" while "Howard served a tour [actually two] in Uganda before returning to England and marrying an heiress."[79]

Macallister's own place of education has not come to light, but his middle class, imperial and clerical background are clearly apparent and he went to East Africa as one of the establishment, unlike James Martin the illiterate from Malta, though perhaps also something of an adventurer.[80]

On the 5th July 1890 he and Burrows signed his contract with the Company and he sailed two days later from London as a first class passenger on the S.S. *Ethiopia* of the British India Steam Navigation Company. Built in 1874, this passenger/cargo vessel of 2,032 tons was newly engaged on the route, which called at Marseilles, Naples, Port Said, Aden (where his grandfather had served for so long), Mombasa, and then on to Zanzibar.[81] His initial three year appointment began as soon as the vessel sailed from London. Salary was set at three hundred and thirty Rupees a month in the first year, rising by a further sixty Rupees in the second year and again in the third. Certainly by 1892–3 his income at £360.p.a. was roughly equivalent to an Engineer in Britain, but with far fewer overheads.

The comparison is relevant for Macallister had trained as an engineer, serving his pupillage under Mr J. A. C. Hay. Afterwards he gained experience in railway construction in Britain before being appointed Executive Engineer in the Company. He was responsible for laying a tramway across Mombasa Island, and with C. W. Hobley he constructed a narrow gauge railway to Maseras, where he discovered some argentiferous galena lodes. He had a continuing interest in rocks and what might be extracted from within them. On 31st August 1894 he

---

[79] Personal communication from the Revd. B. R. McAllister, (who spelt the name thus) 30th August, 1976; and School Lists.

[80] James Martin (1857–1924) the illiterate Maltese, who still illiterate, became a Collector (District Commissioner) in the Uganda Protectorate (see below note 84).

[81] Details from 'The Ships List.'

was appointed an Administrative Officer in the new Uganda Protectorate which was proclaimed four days earlier. Because of his African experience he was appointed a Vice-Consul on the 5th May 1895 and a First Class Assistant.[82]

As for his personality, he must have been physically strong and resilient to have survived in conditions in which some of his contemporaries died prematurely. Moreover his work was effective, for he was selected to pioneer at Port Victoria (later replaced by Kisumu), where he set up the Civil Station, as he would later do in Ankole and then in the Nile Province.

In 1896 a mechanic at Port Victoria, John Anderson Macdonald, charged him with assault, but it is doubtful whether this was anything more than the expression of a personality clash, common enough when a couple of Europeans were thrown together in trying circumstances.[83] A certain stubbornness is also apparent perhaps in Macallister's refusal to be re-examined for the Language allowance "as I passed an examination in Kiswahili by Mr. James Martin... early in 1895", but was afterwards informed that it could not be accepted because "Mr. James Martin could not read or write",[84] and in his resolve to stay on in East Africa in 1905 after his retirement from Government service, despite this having been on medical grounds.

Early in 1897 he went on leave, and during that year he proposed to Mabel Katherine Johnstone, but her father refused

---

[82] Details of his life given here are culled from various sources including *Drumkey's Year Book for East Africa 1904*, and Staff Lists. Mr D. Simpson, Librarian of the Royal Commonwealth Society generously supplied information from the 'Dictionary of East Africa Biography' and the Secretary of the Institute of Civil Engineers similarly provided a copy of an obituary notice from the Institute's *Minutes of Proceedings*, Vol. 179, p. 368. For the first decade the Uganda Protectorate was administered by the Commissioner, Deputy Commissioner, First Class Assistants (Sub-Commissioners, some of who were also Vice-Consuls), Second Class (Collectors), and Third Class Assistants.

[83] Anderson to Commissioner, March 1896: ESA A4/5/114, and Macallister to Commissioner, 12th May 1896, ESA A4/5/138.

[84] Macallister to Ternan, 26th October 1899, ESA A4/22/39.

his consent. Returning to Uganda at the beginning of 1898, he missed the more urgent days of the Mutiny but still qualified to receive the medal. Being one of the most experienced officers at the disposal of the Commissioner (Berkeley), and one of only four First Class Assistants, he went to pioneer in Ankole as Sub-Commissioner, as has already been discussed.

In August 1900 he again received a pioneering role, this time as first Sub-Commissioner for the new Nile Province. Richard Baile, his assistant in Ankole, paid a considerable tribute to him when, after eighteen months together in their own pioneer situation he wrote, "I have not the slightest desire to be transferred to another district. Everything goes along smoothly and I have never had the slightest friction with Mr. Macallister." Locally he was given a name in *Runyankore* which has been explained in this way. "Mr Macallister was a tall and a stout figure, so huge that the Natives feared and nicknamed him the 'Thicket' or 'Shrub' in the vernacular *Kisaka.*"[85]

On his next home leave, in 1901, he proposed again to the same lady. This time her father consented. William Lee Johnstone came from Dringhouses on the edge of York. A landed proprietor all of his life, his independent means were substantial enough to enabled him to raise six children, and to have no occupation. He was now in his early seventies, living as a "gentleman" with his wife, two unmarried daughters and a servant on the edge of Eastbourne.

The couple were married there at St Anne's Church on 6th August 1901, with his brother, Howard, also on leave from the Uganda Administration as best man. His own father came down from Plumstead to conduct the ceremony, and the bride's parents were present and signed the register. Macallis-

---

[85]   R. Baile to J. F. Cunningham 6th May 1900. ESA A/4/28/408. Berkeley seems to have made a happy choice in sending Baile as Macallister's assistant. They had already travelled from the coast together on Baile's first appointment in February, and in August they had gone on safari together to the salt deposit at Usingiri in south Kavirondo on the south side of Ugowe bay. ESA A/4/13/634. I am grateful to Mr. A. G. Katate who gave me the note on the vernacular name *Kishaka*.

ter was styled "Civil Servant" aged thirty-nine and Mabel, a spinster aged thirty-two. He tried to extend his leave on the grounds of ill health but had to leave again for Uganda in November. By then his son had been conceived. He came on leave once more before he left Government service.[86]

His last appointment before retiring on 31st December 1904 was in the Western Province, again as Sub-Commissioner, from which position he was able to observe the very considerable changes which had taken place in Ankole since he had first gone there in a pioneering capacity only a few years previously.[87] Thereafter he made his headquarters in Nairobi.

With hindsight it would be harsh to judge of his marriage, since it was not uncommon for early administrators and others to leave their wives and children in Britain, awaiting their return on the next leave probably two or three years ahead, and was not unknown with expatriates in the 1970s. Nevertheless, in Macallister's case it must have been singularly unsatisfactory for his wife and two children, Brian Robert born in 1902 and Enid Mona born two years later. They can hardly have known their father.

Macallister's death from dysentery on 11th April 1909 somewhere in the Semliki Valley "where he had been prospecting for some time"[88] was perhaps the result of a rather desperate venture, for his son was reared on the story that he "retired from the Government service to make his fortune speculating in land in Uganda." Later "his partner defrauded

---

[86]   Census returns; marriage certificate, etc.

[87]   *General Report on the Uganda Protectorate for the year ending 31 March 1904*, London, H.M.S.O., (Africa No.12, 1904) paragraph 29.

[88]   Item 601/09, ESA B/14/I5. When Macallister died the *East Africa Standard* failed to notice the event, while *The Leader* only gave the briefest mention. Details of his life given here are culled from various sources including *Drumkey's Yearbook for East Africa*, 1904, and Staff lists. Mr. D. Simpson, Librarian of the Royal Commonwealth Society, generously supplied information from the 'Dictionary of East African Biography' and the Secretary of the Institute of Civil Engineers kindly provided a copy of an obituary notice from the Institute's *Minutes of Proceedings,* Vol. 179, p. 368.

him and the transaction fell through. ... My mother got nothing back from Africa, everything was stolen after his death."[89] The former Sub-Commissioner's body was brought in to Fort Portal and buried there. Such was Macallister's tragic end. After his death Mabel continued to live with her children in Eastbourne. She had sufficient means to occupy a six room house, but had no servant, unlike her widowed mother who still lived nearby with her other daughter.

The conclusion on his personality must be that he was an effective administrator who was aware of the mineral potential of the country, but who lost his life in this vain attempt to make a significant discovery, and thus to restore and improve his fortunes. His official career seems to have been unblemished and the possibility that he tried to use his position to use philately for personal gain (see Appendix B) seems somewhat farcical. The suggestion that he was therefore rather dishonest is also belied by the apparently meticulous way in which he reported the finding of potentially exploitable minerals.[90] Moreover, if he was so grasping for money, why did he so stubbornly forgo the language allowance to which he was entitled by refusing to re-take the examination?

---

[89]   Macallister, B.R. *ibid.*

[90]   Curiously enough it was over that particular matter that his brother, Howard, left Uganda under something of a cloud. He was accused of having used knowledge gained while a Government official and selling it to a mineral company for ten thousand pounds, a very large sum at the time. Nothing was admitted or pursued further, but Howard resigned his appointment and returned home (see official correspondence). Was this the origin of the story that he married an heiress? See above note 79.

MACALLISTER, possibly in Mbarara

CHAPTER FIVE

MACALLISTER AND MBARARA
1898–1900

This then was the man who set out with instructions to hold and form a consular court at "Ntali's" or some more suitable station that he might choose in due course.[91] Though Ntare's *orurembo* was located in different places at different times, there can be little doubt that what the British meant by "Ntali's" was in the region of the Muti hills where Ntare had been living during the times when Lugard and Cunningham had made treaties with his representatives, even though there was some uncertainty, especially on maps, as to exactly where it was.

Macallister arrived at Muti on 18th December 1898 and on 1st January 1899 was able to request Berkeley "to appoint Mbarara as the place."[92] The question then arises as to the reasons for the choice of this site. There were three. First of all it was available. Having been vacated by Ntare, it had not been re-occupied as a capital site. There was no question arising over the ownership of the land. Dr Karugire states[93] categorically that "the *Omugabe* owns *everything* in his Kingdom" and as already seen Macallister had not come as a conqueror, but at

---

[91] Berkeley to Macallister, 19th December 1898, ESA A/5/4/319. We have seen that Macallister held a commission as Vice-Consul, hence the reference to a court.

[92] Macallister to Berkeley, 1st January 1899, ESA A/4/I5/19 No.1. Recently (1969) a new road on the edge of the *boma* has been aptly named Muti Drive.

[93] Karugire, *op. cit.* (1971) p. 105; Macallister shows his awareness of this point when writing to Ternan about Land Regulations: "In Ankole all land is the property of the King and chiefs hold land only during his pleasure." ESA A4/9/505 No.18.

the invitation of Kahaya and escorted by Mbaguta. So the land was free to be used for the building of the government station.

Secondly, it was suitable. It had the advantage of a commanding position, and could be defended. There was a perennial water supply and it was centrally situated in the district. The *Omugabe* was currently located reasonably close at hand at Rushasha, and the trade route from German East Africa ran close by, control of trade being an important factor.

Thirdly, it was already known to the British. As we have seen both Lugard and Cunningham had concluded that any post to be established should be "at Ntali's". Therefore there was no need to spend much time in seeking out a suitable place, and Macallister was able to go straight to the spot and commence work. He pitched his tents on the Muti site, appointed it as "the place," and called it Mbarara. At the same time he was able to report that

> I am endeavouring to build a station, and stores, but owing to the scarcity of tools, it will take a considerable time to complete them. A thorn *zereba*, as a temporary measure has been made, and the Europeans, Government stores, and half company of troops are safe in case of a night attack.[94]

Two sites are described here. The *zereba* was on the highest of the three summits of the Muti hills, that is the southerly one. In 1907, Major E. M. Jack (Royal Engineers) of the Anglo-Congolese Boundary Commission wrote a description of Mbarara. With an eye for both military and topographical details he described this hill "on which the first fort that was ever made ... was built."[95] The summit of this certainly provided a commanding defensive position, "devoid as it was of anything but grass"[96] and with an all-round field of fire for about five

---

[94] Macallister to Berkeley, 1st January 1899, ESA A/4/15/20 No.2.

[95] Jack, E. M., *op. cit.* pp. 58–59.

[96] Garstin, Sir W., *Report upon the Basin of the Upper Nile with proposals for the improvement of that river*, Cairo (1904), pp. 34–35. Opposite p, 34 there is a photograph of the fort hill taken early in 1903 (see photograph) on which the slopes are devoid of trees. There is another earthwork, still marked (1970) by a row of seven jacarandas below this summit and roughly to the north (now part of the golf course) which was probably the original lower camp.

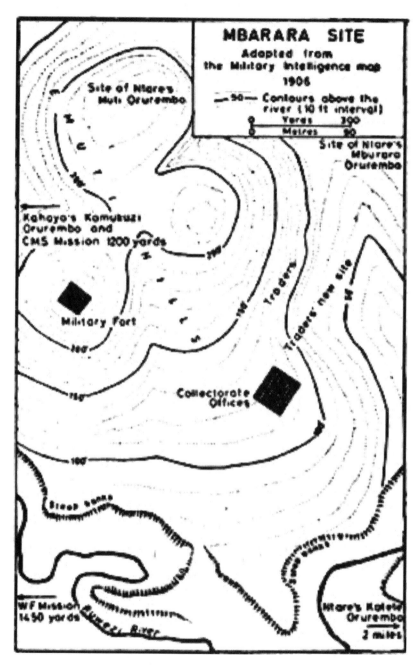

MBARARA SITE PLAN, first published *UJ* (1973) p. 35.

hundred yards, though water from the Ruizi was a little further off. The site of this fort was still (1970) marked by several rather ancient jacarandas which have survived the building of the municipal water tank on this highest point.

The hill top could not have accommodated, even temporarily, the number of men Macallister had with him, and they doubtless camped below the fort, which as it turned out was never needed in earnest. Macallister goes on to describe the second site, which he wisely chose on flatter ground, and which he had already selected for the building of the station and stores:

> The station ground I have selected is on the spur of a hill overlooking the River Ruizi, a stream of about 40 feet wide, and at low water about 4 feet deep, and within half mile of the main road from Kitangoli to Toru, and Unyoro, through Ankole. The King's village is about 3 hours distant, the climate should be healthy and there is a large population of natives, both *Wanyoro* and *Wahima*.[97]

Clearly this is the area enclosed by a ditch which can still be seen (1970) between the present prison and D.C.'s Office, and is described in the Government Handbook for 1913: "The original *boma* was built well down on the slopes of the hill ... by the site of an old kraal of Ntale."[98] It is in fact situated to the south of the southerly summit, whereas Ntare's *kraal* had been on the eastern slopes of the northern summit, a few hundred yards away, about opposite the later Grindlays Bank building.[99]

---

[97]   Macallister to Berkeley, 1st January 1899, ESA A/4/15/20 No.2. The '*Wanyoro*' here means the '*Bairu*' as Macallister makes clear later. The *Omugabe* was then at Rushasha, about 10 miles out on the Fort Portal road.

[98]   *Uganda handbook,* Entebbe, G.P., (1913), p. 52. This *boma* site was marked by a concrete cone about 1940. It bore a metal plate inscribed simply "SITE OF FIRST GOVERNMENT STATION OF MBARARA OCCUPIED 1898." *Uganda Herald,* 11th November 1942. This has been missing for some years. If the cone is still there, it is a pity that it is not re-marked, as the inscription simply states a fact which should be beyond dispute. When in Uganda, the writer had a friend with the difficult task of Conservator of Antiquities for the country.

[99]   Katate and Kamugungunu, *op. cit.* Bk. 1, p. 143.

MACALLISTER'S LETTER

MACALLISTER'S LETTER written to Berkeley, the Commissioner and Consul-General, appointing "Mbarara as the place" for setting up his court as Vice-Consul and official representative of Queen Victoria

Though his account dates from 1907, Major Jack is worth quoting at length because his descriptions are very evocative of the atmosphere of those early days in Mbarara. There may be better ones tucked away in family letters and reminiscences both in Uganda and in Britain, but these have not come to light, whereas his are readily available in print but may not be known to readers. He has a careful description of the head-quarters and centre of the Protectorate Government. He comments that such places usually coincide

> with the position of the fort, as not so many years ago existence was somewhat precarious in these outlying parts, and one had to be prepared for all eventualities. At Mbarara the *boma* is formed actually by the ditch of the old fort, and one enters it by a gateway by a guard-house. ... Inside ... you see facing you a low, square building, heavily thatched, its walls built of sun-dried bricks – in other words mainly of mud – and roughly whitewashed, the windows closed by shutters and innocent of glass, the whole dark, dusty and dirty.[100]

The Administrator lived there, that is straight ahead of anyone entering, while to the right was

> another mud-built house, considerably larger, but otherwise very similar to the living-house just described; this is the Government office, comprising under the one roof the offices of the District and Assistant Commissioners, the post-office, and a large room used as a store.[101]

He describes seeing witnesses, friends and spectators around the central door which is of the court-house where a case (of "which there is a never ending supply"[102]) is being heard. Another group is of porters about to start for Kampala under "the *nyampara* or headman". Outside another door which is for the post-office, its police sentry is sitting on a bench. He is talking to "an individual in blue and red stripes here and there who is the postman." Then he takes us inside:

> a low, rather dark room, with two large Chubb's safes against the wall. At each window near the light is a table

---

[100]   Jack, *op. cit.*, pp. 53–54.

[101]   *Ibid*, p. 54.

[102]   *Ibid*, p. 55 (and for the next three quotes).

'MBARARA HEADQUARTERS' Garstin's photograph of 1903, showing the fort on the hill top with a few trees, and camp lines below on the left

'KATWE FORT' from a watercolour by Bishop Tucker, an Artist who exhibited at the Royal Academy before he trained for the ministry. This photograph shows his view of Fort George at Katwe and, though more elaborate than that at Mbarara, it gives a clearer impression of a British fort.

covered with papers. Round the room are roughly made shelves, cup-boards, and pigeon-holes, containing other books and papers. All are covered with a fine dust.

In a storm the shutters are closed, leaving those inside in darkness. The postmaster is "Mr Pereira, a Goanese, who is also the Government office clerk. ... Intelligent, hard-working, and trustworthy."[103]

At the other table you may see the native interpreter, Sedulaka, seated ... a jewel among natives. He speaks excellent English, is most intelligent and reliable ... really almost indispensible ... modest and unaffected. ... Long may he live!

So much for what is to be seen inside the *boma* "except when mails come in." This postal service

leaves Entebbe for Mbarara every Monday evening and arrives on Thursday morning, having traversed the distance of 150 miles in three nights and two days. The whole journey is done on foot, in relays of course, and the speed and regularity of the delivery speak well for the organization of the post. ... Two or three runners bustle in, bearing the mail-bags on their heads. The bags are taken over, opened, and the contents strewn on the floor ... and Mr Pereira sorts them out. ... A boy is probably waiting from the Protestant Mission to take their letters; a French Father arrives on his bicycle, his white robe tucked up round his waist; there is an orderly from the King's African Rifles detachment, and sundry Indian traders and natives waiting. Each takes his packet of letters and is off; there remain, perhaps, some for natives, the addresses not always easy to decipher; the names are called out to the waiting crowd, and the owner, if not there is hurriedly sent for; so the delivery is completed.[104]

Having concluded his description of what was to be seen within the *boma*, Jack then takes us outside to a

wide stretch of bare earth which is the police parade-ground. ... At the end furthest from the *boma* is a brick-building, which is the baraza or council-hall, used for important or ceremonious occasions, when the District Com-

---

[103]   *Ibid*, p. 56 (and for the next two quotes).

[104]   *Ibid*, pp. 56–57.

missioner … meet[s] the *Mugabe* and the chiefs in *baraza*. This hall was built in Memory of Mr Galt. … On one side of the parade ground is the prison and the police-superintendent's office; in front you see the police sentry standing, a smartly turned out native in khaki with a red cummerbund. Nearby are the police barracks … A body of men armed and trained as soldiers, mainly from local natives and *Baganda*, but including also a certain number of Sudanese. They are an excellent force.[105]

Two matters of interest can be pointed out. Traces of a good deal of what Jack describes here were still evident in 1970, though the Galt Memorial Hall (as it had become) seemed, perhaps, rather small for its purpose, but that may just be a reflection of changed times. It is interesting to see also how far the police had become "Ugandanised" in half a dozen years. At the outset there were no police and only Sudanese troops.

As for the houses for the few Europeans, he describes the contrast between the coveted "comfort and coolness of the old mud-built quarter" despite being rather dark and dirty [lacking window glass], and the new brick-built dwellings with corrugated iron roofs which became intolerably hot and lacked the wide thatched verandahs, so that officials "fervently hoped they would not be 'modernised'."[106]

"Like Rome", Jack finds Mbarara to be a settlement built on hills so that the royal residence was to be found on another, much as described by others. Near it was Mbaguta's house and "also the native *baraza* hall. In the latter most cases dealing with native matters are tried. …"[107] We shall quote his vivid descriptions of more of the early days of Mbarara in other chapters.

Muti possessed several advantages as a site for a station, and the future town, including its commanding position near the river which could be forded and later bridged, and its location at an emerging route centre on the road from Toro to German East Africa (Tanzania). The ability to control such

---

[105] *Ibid*, pp. 57–58.

[106] *Ibid*, pp. 59 & 58.

[107] *Ibid*, p. 60.

trade as already existed had been a factor in its choice. Though the traditional kingdom of Nkore was not synonymous with the British creation of modern Ankole, Muti is nonetheless central in both, a decided advantage when travel was on foot, but of more than passing significance.

The reference to a large population of natives is interesting, and certainly food supply was to cause problems in the initial years of the growing community as Lugard had foreseen. Under Macallister and early in 1900, Fisher and most of the troops had to leave Mbarara temporarily in order to find food elsewhere.[108] Later in the same year, a month after Macallister's departure in August, Herbert Clayton commented:

> Food is very scarce at Mbarara. There are so many people in connection with the Europeans to be fed, a company of Sudanese soldiers, some 130 police, porters, boys, etc. There is no cultivation round the capital but only the cow *kraals*, where the king and his chiefs and their attendants live, and all the food has to be brought in from these same hills.[109]

This is not the description of a resident, but of someone then only coming to Mbarara and then travelling on to and from Rushasha. It does not provide evidence of the adjacent areas.

A year later (July 1901) one of the first C.M.S. missionaries in the area, J. J. Willis, could be an outspoken critic of officials. He wrote that:

> It would not be exactly easy to say why they ever selected Mbarara as the capital. The more one journeys about, the more one is impressed with the fact that they seem to have hit on the one spot in all Ankole where you have to march a whole day or two days before you come on any cultivation worth the name."[110]

---

[108] Macallister to H. H. Johnston, 8th January 1900, Mbarara C/1, ESA A/4/25/37.

[109] H. Clayton in letter to family in U.K., (hereafter C.L.) 17th September 1900. Photostat copies of these letters are at Makerere. Four weeks before there had been only forty-five police (see note 123). Perhaps he confused numbers of police and of troops in a Company of soldiers, or recruitment may have been rapid.

[110] Willis, J. J. 'Journal', (hereafter W.J.) 30th July 1901. Copies are held

This comment is carefully observed six months after arriving in Mbarara. Eighteen months earlier, Macallister had reported "a large population" of both pastoralists (*Wahima*) and cultivators (*Wanyoro*, but actually *Bairu*). The first could subsist where there was only water and grass, deriving all nutriment from their cattle, but not so the agriculturalists. Without local cultivation they would always have been dependent on supplies from further afield.

However this food problem could be remedied. Mbaguta, who is well remembered for his vigorous encouragement of cultivation, said in a statement made about the end of 1905 that, "Before the establishment of a Government station at Mbarara there were severe famines in the country. These are becoming yearly less severe."[111]

There can be no doubt that Macallister chose the Muti site for his headquarters. Why then did he call it by another name? The reason for him appointing "Mbarara as the place" must have been due to a slight confusion resulting from his enquiries about the location of "Ntali's". The last site in the immediate vicinity occupied by this *Omugabe* was Mburara, while Macallister was now establishing himself adjacent to an earlier *orurembo* of Ntare V at Muti.

The corruption of the name to Mbarara is usually blamed on the inability of the first European officials to get names

---

in Lambeth Palace Library & at Makerere. On the question of bridging the Ruizi river, there was no permanent structure until 1929, but Sir John Gray, *op. cit.* pp.47-48 quotes Sir A. Kaggwa, *Basekabaka b'e Buganda,* p.164 (speaking of the activities of the Christian exiles in Ankole) "Ntare also sent us to bridge rivers and we bridged one very large river." Gray comments that, "the bridge, or rather embankment, was constructed across the Ruizi River close to the present township of Mbarara. Though *Baganda* appear to have been noted for their ability to construct such works, a causeway of this description was a novelty in Ankole. When some eight years later cattle raiders from Rwanda reached the river, they thought the embankment must have been constructed by Europeans." There is no indication of anything except fords and wooden bridges on the 1906 map.

[111]   A. H. Watson to Commissioner, Mbarara, 25th January 1906, ESA A/15/2.

right, and for which Willis also took them to task.[112] This is very probably the case, and not so surprising when they spoke only *Swahili* and were dealing with an unknown language which was not written. It is a little surprising, perhaps, to find *Banyankole* historians speaking of Ntare's site and using the same corrupted name, though it shows that the corruption had now become acceptable.[113] At all events there has been a permanent settlement here bearing this name since the very end of the nineteenth century. Moreover, it is more than fitting that the name is derived from *mburara*, the red-oat grass favoured by the *Bahima* for their cattle, since there was little else when Macallister arrived. The front cover shows traditional terrain.

Indeed, the official guide compiled a dozen years later retrospectively states that Mbarara

> is in the middle of a wide expanse of undulating short grass pasture land. Formerly there was practically no cultivation near at hand, and food had to be transported from the hill country some distance away.[114]

The development of Mbarara during the early months of 1899 can be considered with respect to four functions – (i) European administration, including troops, (ii) native administration which was soon to be located there, (iii) trade and (iv) missionary activity. This will reveal how much had been achieved during Macallister's time, and that these activities had arisen as a result of the setting up of a Government station at this place.

The European administration really commenced with Macallister's arrival at the site on 18th December 1898. There is no record of his third-class assistant, Richard Baile arriving later, and so clearly they travelled together as Berkeley had intended. Nor is there any record of who the other Europeans were in the party,[115] though from Macallister's reports during

---

[112] W.J., 24th October 1902, quoted in M. Doornbos, *UJ*, **30**, 1966, p. 210.

[113] Katate and Kamugungunu, *op. cit.* Bk. 1, p. 156. The Muti *orurembo* was on top of the northern summit by the rocky outcrop above Johnston road. Personal communication from Mr A. G. Katate.

[114] *Handbook*, p. 52 – see note 98.

[115] Berkeley to Baile, 29th October 1898, ESA A/5/4/256.

the following weeks it is certain that Captain A. A. Fisher (West Yorks Regt) was commanding the troops of No. 6 Company, Uganda Rifles, and that Lieutenant H. C. Moorhouse (Royal Artillery) was with him.[116] Clearly these then were the "four European officials in Ankole" mentioned by the missionary, Clayton, as he closely watched the developing situation from neighbouring Koki. [117]

The state of the country was fairly disturbed, due partly to the presence of Nubian and *Baganda* 'rebels', and also to the internal conflict among leading *Bahinda*, especially between Igumira and Kahitsi. Most of the time the troops seemed to remain in Mbarara, occasionally sallying forth on expeditions and forays. This unrest did not prevent the Government station being developed on the 'spur' site selected by Macallister at the beginning though there were other difficulties. In the middle of 1900 Baile looked back on this time and wrote:

> I attribute my bad health some time back to the hard work and anxiety of getting the station built. We had no carpenter or handy-man of any sort, so that not only had I to superintend the building but actually to do all the work myself such as making doors, windows, etc.[118]

A couple of months earlier Macallister had reported to the Special Commissioner:

> Several buildings are required, but as there is not a carpenter nothing can be done. ... I was told when leaving Kampala that the first carpenter arriving from the coast would be sent after me, but he has not arrived here yet [i.e. eighteen months later].

Ironically enough, it was three days after Macallister left Mbarara that the first "two artisans named Bachoo Abdullah and Juma Ferhani, one a carpenter, the other a mason" arrived. In the same letter he also stated that

---

[116] Macallister to Ternan, 2nd June 1899, ESA A/4/7/26, – in his letter from Kajuna, Buddu, 18th January 1899 Clayton wrote: "At Masaka I found a large staff of Europeans. There was one officer who is going on to Ankole." From the context this was a military officer, and was probably Moorhouse.

[117] C. L., Koki, 23rd March 1899.

[118] Baile to Cunningham, 6th May 1900, ESA A/4/28/408.

A compounder [someone who mixes medicines] or hospital assistant, if a doctor is not available, is also required, as at certain times of the year there is considerable sickness among the troops and native staff.[119]

In fact, in the Protectorate Estimates for 1900–01 printed in February 1900, before this letter was written, "one hospital assistant and one hospital attendant"[120] were included. There is no indication that either ever arrived, and in the following year the estimate is altered to "one Medical Officer only."[121] Not until May 1902 did Dr Ralph Stoney arrive as the first M.O.[122]

In the early part of August 1900, a week or two before Macallister left, Sir Harry Johnston, the Special Commissioner, had paid a visit to the station. Throughout the Protectorate he considered that "the troops had been given too much police work" and was planning to restore a really civil administration now that peace had been restored after the disturbances arising from the Mutiny. His scheme to set up a native constabulary "trained by sergeants of the Metropolitan police and the regular army" is reflected in the fact that when Macallister left, Racey was able to report that forty-five men had been enlisted and "The English sergeant, to whom you referred when here, would now be of the greatest service in training these men. ..."[123]

Mr Lazaro Kamugungunu, who was *Enganzi* of Ankole from 1938 to 1946, was the joint author of a book in the vernacular on the history of the kings of Ankole which has al-

---

[119] Macallister to Johnston, 9th March 1900, ESA A/4/26/199. Also Ankole Report, see note 5 p. 31.

[120] Uganda Protectorate Estimates, 1900–01, pp. 6.

[121] Uganda Protectorate Estimates, 1901–02, pp. 9.

[122] Moffat, R. U., *P.M.O.'s Report,* 1903, p. 15, M.O.H. Library, Entebbe. The Estimates had a result: "At the Fort they have just received a complete medical outfit of about 13 loads, containing all sorts of drugs, surgical instruments, chloroform, etc. They suppose therefore that a medical officer is to be appointed here, though they have not heard anything about it for there are quantities of things which would be of no use to anyone but a doctor." (C.L. 18th May 1901).

[123] Moyse-Bartlett, *op. cit.,* p. 83; also Racey to Johnston, 23rd August 1900, ESA A/15/1/14.

ready been quoted. He "first saw Mbarara in about 1900 and remembers the place consisting of a small camp made up of [the Collector's] office and house, both of which were built of mud, and thatched with grass and surrounded for protection by the Sudanese troops' barracks."[124]

Dr Lowsley, in his 1906 report speaks of the "civil quarters which are mud built, grass roofed, old and dark, and are I believe shortly to be replaced."[125] In the following year. Major Jack, gives a full description of these original buildings, and of the Government Office and Post Office which was not built until about 1901–02.[126] Such were the small beginnings of the administration.

Macallister left Mbarara on 21st August 1900 "to proceed to the Nile Provinces."[127] During his twenty months as Sub-Commissioner in Ankole there were few changes and no fatalities among the European personnel. Among the civil staff, Baile remained for almost the whole period, only leaving for Toro in June 1900 when R. R. Racey arrived to replace him. Baile had acquired the title of Collector under Johnston's re-organization, and when Macallister, departed, Racey remained as Collector for the district, coming under the Sub-Commissioner for the Western Province. V. M. Manara was a Maltese who arrived as the Government clerk during 1900, and because of his ability was soon made Assistant Collector (April 1901). On the military side, Captain Fisher remained as O.C. Troops until April 1900. Then in about the middle of 1899 Moorhouse was replaced by Lieutenant G. C. R. Mundy (Leicester Regt) who was left in sole military charge when Fisher went on leave and was not replaced because of the war in South Africa.[128]

---

[124] Ntare School History Society, 'The development of the town of Mbarara', typescript, (1970), p. 2.

[125] Lowsley, L. D., 'Supplementary Annual Medical Report; Ankole District 1906', p. 4, in the P.M.O.'s Report, M.O.H. Library, Entebbe.

[126] See above note 100.

[127] Macallister, R. J. D., 'Report for Ankole, August 1900', ESA A/15/1/9.

[128] To expatriates, the human cost was high. Three of these seven died within a few years because of their time in Africa: Baile on 16th

By the time Macallister was moved on, Mbarara was sufficiently established for it to be left, at least for some months, in
the hands of only one British administrator and one army officer.

Note on the First Medical Officers

Those like Dr Parke (see Appendix A), who were accompanying expeditions passing through Nkore do not concern us. Dr
Cook (afterwards Sir Albert) was doing rather more than that,
but very briefly. He came from his life's work at Mengo, together with Bishop Tucker, on a missionary reconnaissance in
1899. That certainly had the *Banyankore* and their needs firmly in mind.

During this chapter, we have seen scientific medical work
established. It was part of, and depended on, the Protectorate
administration. Something more can be said here of the first
three doctors.

Ralph Stoney (1863–1905) originated in Tipperary, Ireland,[129] but in 1899 came to East Africa from Kensington in
London, where he left his wife and young daughter during his
tours of duty overseas. Having served elsewhere, he arrived in
Mbarara in May 1903 and only ten months later went on home
leave.[130] His journeying shows something of the inefficient use
of manpower caused by travel. It was a month before he sailed
from Mombasa, and was not back in Mbarara until the following January.[131] In mid July he was posted to Bunyoro.[132] It was
while there that he was killed by an elephant when out shoot-
ing, on 19th October 1905. His only daughter grew up to quali-
fy as a solicitor, unusual in those days.

March 1901 at Kisumu on the way to the coast at the end of his first
tour; Fisher on 12th March 1902 after having returned home from
service in South Africa; and Macallister in 1909. However, Sir Harry
Moorhouse ended a long career in Africa as Lieutenant Governor of
Southern Nigeria.

[129] *Burke's Landed Gentry of Ireland* (1958) p. 658.

[130] C. L. 10th March 1903.

[131] C. L. 17th February 1904.

[132] C. L. (10th) 7th July 1904.

Alexander McCarthy-Morrogh (1864–1927) was from county Cork, also in Ireland.[133] Having previously worked in Nyasaland, he came to Uganda in 1900. He was posted to Mbarara from "sleeping sickness duty" at Entebbe and the Sese Islands, and arrived about the 6th March 1903[134] just in time to replace Stoney. After a stay of more than a year he was replaced and resigned on account of ill-health, leaving Uganda in November 1904. The P.M.O., Moffat said "he was a decent sort of Irishman and very amusing."[135]

Lionel Dewe Lowsley (1866–1936) was a different kind of replacement. When he arrived in Mbarara in mid July 1904[136] he was accompanied by his wife and four year old son. This must have been the first European child to live in Ankole. Moreover Lowsley stayed for much of the next four years. During that time two more children were born and baptised by Clayton. He served in East Africa from 1902–1916 when he had to retire on medical grounds. Curiously, he was returning to East Africa when he died at Mombasa on the eve of his seventieth birthday. The young son became a Colonel in the Gurkhas and was killed in the Second World War.

All three of these doctors came with considerable medical experience elsewhere. More curiously, perhaps, all three were from landed families. Lowsley was of the The Manor House, Hampstead Norreys in Berkshire, though two of his brothers were also doctors and another a clergyman. He and his son were at the same school as that eventually attended by the writer. The family had given him a photograph (since destroyed) showing the Lowsleys together on a picnic near Mbarara in about 1906, much as we would later enjoy doing ourselves – but without the *solar topee*!

---

[133] Burke, *op. cit.*, p. 509.

[134] C.L. even date.

[135] Foster, W. D. *The Early History of Scientific Medicine in Uganda, Nairobi*, (1970) p. 35.

[136] C. L. (10th) 7th July and 21st July 1904. See also *Burke's Landed Gentry* for those years.

CHAPTER SIX

RE-LOCATION OF THE INDIGENOUS ADMINISTRATION TO MBARARA

The development of native administration may now be reviewed. When Macallister arrived in Ankole he found Kahaya as *Omugabe,* but with Igumira and Kahitsi as "his principal chiefs," and later he learnt that these two "have acted as Regents until quite recently." From the first he formed the opinion that Kahaya was anxious to co-operate, but "being very young, I fear he is much in the hands of his chiefs." Igumira and Kahitsi were outwardly friendly but Macallister was suspicious of Kahitsi, who had "supported Mwanga's party in the past, and is in league with the powder-runners."[137] Moreover, as Dr. Karugire points out, by this time Kahitsi had withdrawn his support from Kahaya and was backing a rival candidate, Rwakatogoro.[138]

As soon as Macallister arrived in Mbarara
Kahitsi promptly appealed to him not to recognize Kahaya, and, to ensure sympathetic support, he offered his sister, Kyabatuku, to Macallister in marriage. To the consternation of everyone, except perhaps the prospective bridegroom, Macallister declined the offer rather rudely. The latter, moreover, was already definitely on Kahaya's side, but this did not influence his decision to decline Kahitsi's offer.[139]

This kind of reporting of the episode shows a lack of understanding of both the African and European reactions to such an offer. It is obvious that Kahaya and his supporters were not

---

[137] Macallister to Berkeley, 1st January 1899, ESA A/4/15/20 No.2, and Macallister to Ternan, 10th July 1899, ESA A/4/19/469.

[138] See notes 66 and 71.

[139] Karugire, *op. cit.,*(1971) pp. 249–250.

'THE KING OF ANKOLE AND HIS COUNSELLORS'
Viewed left to right: Mbaguta, Kahaya, Igumira, and Kahitsi.

in the least disconcerted by Macallister's refusal, while he can never for a moment have thought that it was any part of his official duty as one of Queen Victoria's Vice-Consuls to enter into a marriage with an African princess, and it is inconceivable that he should ever have thought of accepting what must have seemed to him an outrageous proposition.

In the following months Kahitsi was the cause of considerable concern, and by the middle of 1899 the Sub-Commissioner also considered that "Egumira would cause trouble if he saw the slightest chance of success."[140] During this time there was obviously considerable suspicion on both sides. With Kahaya living "about three hours distant" at Rushasha, and coming in to Mbarara "with 500 to 600 spearmen and 50 guns"[141] it must have been difficult for Macallister to know what was really happening in the district.

Doubtless it was for this reason that he wanted to get the *Omugabe* settled much closer to the Government station, and decided to attempt this soon after he had established himself.

---

[140] Macallister to Ternan, 19th June 1899, ESA A/4/18/343.

[141] Macallister to Berkeley, 1st January 1899, ESA A/4/15/20 No.2.

In April Macallister complained of Fisher and the troops being ordered off to Kabula, "thus upsetting my arrangements for getting Kawia in here."[142] A couple of weeks later, writing about early missionary activity, he commented, "would not be surprised to hear that Kawia had fled to German Mpororo, as he has his father's superstitions I read of all white men, and missionaries in particular."[143] However, by the end of May, Kahaya had sufficiently overcome these fears both to have received a European missionary (Clayton) and to have agreed to move. "Here all is peace, Kawia is coming to live near the station, against the advice of many of his elders."[144] Now the *Omugabe* was beginning to act independently of the former regents, and in the direction indicated by the *Enganzi*, Mbaguta. On 19th June 1899 Macallister reported:

> Kawia, with a large following, is now living within a mile
> of the station ... (he) has got over his superstitious fear, and
> has reduced his bodyguard from 500 to 50 men, in fact I
> can safely say that confidence is established,

and a month later "No trouble is anticipated from the *Waankole*, who now acknowledge Kawiya, with the exception of about 100 followers of Kiyisi [Kahitsi]. The district can be held with one company of troops."[145]

As is well known, the site which Kahaya now came to occupy in Mbarara was the hill, Kamukuzi. Though probably not evident at the time, this event in June 1899 marked a radical break with the past. This was the beginning of the location of the *Omugabe*'s court in one place, lasting throughout the reign of Kahaya, and also that of his successor right up to the abolition of the kingdom in 1967. At first there was no significant change. Bishop Tucker and Doctor Cook visited this '*lulembo*' in December 1899, and the former noted that

> our first view of the native capital of Nkole was disappoint-
> ing, to say the least it is little better than a huge cattle *kraal*.

---

142   Macallister to Ternan, 27th April 1899, ESA A/4/17/190.

143   Macallister to Ternan, 8th May 1899, ESA A/4/16/188.

144   Macallister to Ternan, 2nd June 1899, E'SA, A/4/17/264a.

145   Macallister to Ternan, 19th June 1899, ESA A/4/18/343 and 16th July 1899, ESA A/4/19/470.

The King and his dependents live inside the *kraal* with the cattle. The lodging of his majesty is not much better than that of his herds. A thorn *boma* surrounds the whole enclosure. Happily our tents had been pitched, not inside the king's *kraal*, but in the enclosure of the *Katikiro*, some three or four hundred yards away. The *Katikiro* is a 'progressive' and had built his house after the *Luganda* model. We are therefore fairly comfortable.[146]

Once again it is Mbaguta who represented change and who set the pattern for the future; for within two years of moving to Kamukuzi the *Omugabe* had "built himself a large two-storied brick house of which he is very proud."[147] This is presumably further described in a later account:

The palace consists of a large thatched hut, with a collection of smaller ones for the king's women and his suite. These huts are surrounded by a high reed fence, and all over the hill are banana plantations. The English mission church is also situated on this hill. [148]

For sixty-eight years Kamukuzi would remain the first permanent royal capital, within the District of Ankole centred at the on-going 'city' of Mbarara, and now in the smaller district of that name.

---

[146] Tucker, A. R. 'A missionary journey through Nkole', *Church Missionary Intelligencer,* (1900), p. 502.

[147] C. L., 21st April 1901.

[148] Garstin, *op. cit.* p. 35.

CHAPTER SEVEN

TRADE

The development of trade during the early months of 1899 may now be discussed. Traders of a kind were of course already active in the area, and one of the reasons for the setting up of a Government station was to control the traffic in powder, cartridges, and ivory across the German boundary, and to prevent trade in slaves. Among Macallister's first reports is one for 23 December 1898 on the arrest of a *"Swahili,* Mzee bin Suliman, at 10 p.m. in Kiyisi's village"[149] for having suspect items in his possession. However he quickly admitted his inability to do much to control this kind of activity from Mbarara, "it being absolutely impossible to watch every road leading from Toro and Unyoro into German territory."[150] Eventually plans were made to set up two posts in the south of Ankole.

During the first six months of 1899 Macallister was mainly taken up with political matters and establishing the administration. At the end of this period, he noted under the heading 'Resources' that

> Cattle and ivory are at present alone of any value, the former are numerous, but like the Masai and other similar tribes the *Wahima* do not care to sell them. Ivory is scarce, there being I believe only two herds of elephants in Ankole.

He then goes on to describe the agricultural produce of the *Whiro* [*Bairu*], and the fish which "are not eaten, they are dried, and used as a medium of exchange with neighbouring

---

[149] Macallister to Berkeley, 1 January 1899, ESA A/4/15/20 No.2.

[150] Macallister to Berkeley, 22 February 1899, ESA A/4/15/107. For an interesting note on the activity of Muslim traders in Ankole see Y. K. Bamunoba, 'Note on Islam in Ankole', *Dini Na Mila*, Vol. 1, no. 2, September 1965, p. 61.

tribes."[151] At the end of the half year, the revenue return showed an income from trade (Customs on imports and exports) of only Rs 457.12. (less than £30).[152] As the soldiers, and other Government employees were paid in trade goods, there was very little opportunity for commerce as such.

There were no startling changes in the second half of 1899, but the problem of controlling trade in the district as a whole was forcibly impressed on Macallister during a journey he made into northwest Ankole in the second half of September.

> It appears that there is a very considerable trade in ivory from the south end of lake Albert Edward, (where elephants are very numerous), all of which escapes duty, the caravans entering the protectorate near lake Karengi, and passing through Niamizi to the lake. For some time I have suspected the existence of this trade from German territory, as the trading passes issued at Bukoba up to October number 547, whereas only 17 caravans have passed through Mbarara. No doubt many of the caravans went into Buddu, but the majority are trading for ivory, and would naturally go to the cheapest and nearest market.[153]

Dr Karugire agrees that "there was no market" in Ankole. This led Macallister to two conclusions about trade in his area. Firstly, that other customs posts must be set up apart from the one at the station, and secondly, that "a trader should be encouraged to open a store here for the sale of trade goods, and the purchase of ivory."[154]

Macallister was in no doubt that in this second conclusion lay the answer to the problem. Writing to the new Special Commissioner, Sir Harry Johnston, two days after Christmas 1899, he set out five advantages of having a trader settled at Mbarara. (i) The export from Ankole would pass through this trader, thus making collection of duty simple, especially in view of the shortage of suitable staff to collect it; (ii) with a market on the spot, the *Banyankole* would have little incentive

---

[151] Macallister to Ternan, 10 July 1899, ESA A/4/19/469 (both quotes).

[152] *Ibid.*

[153] Macallister to Ternan, 16th October 1899, ESA A/4/22/883.

[154] Karugire, *op. cit.,* (1971) p. 41 and Macallister to Johnston, 27th December 1899, ESA A/4/23/1045.

to continue taking ivory through into German territory for disposal; (iii) the same would be true of trade from the south end of Lakes Albert and Edward; (iv) trade would even be encouraged to pass through Mbarara from the west of Lake Albert Edward and Kitakwenda in the south of Toro, if fair prices were paid; (v) by paying soldiers and native staff in rupees instead of goods, trade in Mbarara would be encouraged and the cost of transporting the goods from Kampala would be removed.[155]

There follows an interesting list of the trade goods which the trader should stock: *americani* (cotton cloth originally from the U.S.A.), "European clothes (cheap coats and trousers)," *vitambi* (lengths of cloth used for making head wear), *vikoi* (white loin cloths with coloured borders), *kanzus* (long robes, usually white), *Kaniki* (dark blue calico or cotton worn as a dress by women), "brass and copper wire, (the latter fine)," "*Ukuta* beads", "knives, scissors, razors, looking glasses, etc."

Strangely enough, when this letter reached Johnston he had already been informed by "two traders, Messrs Chambers and Ormsby" that they were "about to proceed to Ankole and Toro to buy ivory and trade in other things," so he replied by return. Both administrators were somewhat suspicious of the honesty of traders, and Johnston warned his Sub-Commissioner to be

> on your guard against these traders. They may be for all I know the most estimable people in the world, but I never trust traders especially those of my own nationality. They are always striving to obtain some undue advantage out of the Government or out of the inhabitants of these countries.[156]

Nevertheless he was prepared to support the idea of a trader becoming established at Mbarara, and promised that "the first applicant like this firm that arrived on the spot would receive from me a grant of not more than 100 acres of land on a long lease, free of rent, provided the place was chosen for and

---

[155] Macallister to Johnston, 27th December 1899, ESA A/4/23/1045.

[156] Johnston to Macallister, 9th January 1900, ESA A/5/9/23.

used as a trading settlement."[157]

Ormsby was *persona grata* with the Government as he had already been employed by Ternan in 1897 as a Transport Officer for operations against the Nandi and in Buddu, and he was well known to Frederick Jackson.[158] When he arrived in Mbarara on 6th February, Macallister approved a site, selected by him according to Johnston's terms.[159] Thereafter things moved fairly rapidly. In May a market was established which proved to be

> a great success, sheep are killed daily, and salt, grain and vegetables, are brought in large quantities, thus doing away with the necessity for foraging parties, and complaints by natives as a natural consequence. Rupees are in circulation, but native traders are required. I hope by the end of next month [July 1900] to have one, if not two traders established here.[160]

A week after writing this Macallister was requesting the stopping of "all trade goods to Ankole for payment of wages and rations to employees of the Administration, as there are three traders in the district to whom encouragement should be given." At the same time he asked for "a monthly Uganda price list" which "will be a check on trader's prices, and enable me to reckon the correct import dues, at present I have to trust the word of the trader, or trust to my memory." [161]

In fact it was that same month, June 1900, that two *Swahili* traders settled at Mbarara, "but owing to the troops being paid

---

[157]   *Ibid.* This undertaking accords strangely with the acknowledgement that "In Ankole all land is the property of the King" – see note 93.

[158]   Thomas, H. B. 'On the frontiers of another world', *UJ*, 31/1 (1967); p. 123. Another source for Ormsby's activities in Ankole at this time is a fragment from his letter dated 'Mbarara 30 March 1900' written into a family memorial volume in Rhodes House Library, Oxford, under MSS Afr. r. 105. Sir Frederick Jackson (1860-1929) had entered the service of the I.B.E.A.Co. in 1889 and then the Uganda administration in the 1890s. After working elsewhere, he returned to Uganda as Governor from 1911–1917.

[159]   Macallister to Johnston, 12th February, ESA A/4/25/122.

[160]   Macallister to Johnston, 1st June 1900, No.C/17, ESA A/4/28/496.

[161]   Macallister to Johnston, 7th June 1900, No.C/18, ESA A/4/29/536.

primarily in cloth, and the reduction of the native staff, they are heavily handicapped."[162] Nor was this the only problem for "the traders in Ankole, although anxious to buy, have no rupees owing to the issue of cloth as pay to the troops and others," and Macallister wanted "traders from Kampala to come here and buy for the Uganda market" and concludes that in any case "it is hardly fair to the traders who have been induced to settle on the understanding that the employees would be paid in specie."[163]

These traders were settled on a road near the *boma*. They began in tents, but eighteen months later when Galt, the Collector, moved this road further southeast and the bazaar moved with it, he wrote of the traders that, "the buildings already erected by them were only tumble-down shanties." It is a reflection of the progress made and of the cosmopolitan nature of the enterprise that by that time there were "now one European, one Persian, one Arab, one *Swahili* and three Indian firms" carrying on trade.[164] Two European representatives of the Italian Colonial Trading Company were also visiting the place at this time.[165] The activities on the spot were carried on mainly by *Swahili* or Asian agents of these firms.

Thus even before Macallister ceased to be Sub-Commissioner for the district the beginnings of real commercial activity and the use of money were already apparent, even though the difficulties of establishing these were still considerable. Nevertheless, within half a dozen years, there is extraordinary sophistication about the picture painted by Major Jack in his eulogistic account of a few of the better class *duka*.

> The eye wanders round the well filled shelves and fondly *dwells on* the luxuries here displayed, mostly in tins. One sees Russian caviar and Cadbury's chocolates; sardines in tomato and otherwise; French asparagus and solid British steak-and-kidney pies; crystallized fruits cheek by jowl with sliced bacon and sausages. Visions of gorgeous feasts

---

[162] Macallister to Johnston, 5th July 1900, ESA A/4/29/641.

[163] Macallister to Johnston, 30th June 1900, ESA A/4/29/640.

[164] H. St. G. Galt to F. J. Jackson, 2nd November 1901, ESA A/15/2/80.

[165] Racey, R. R., 'Report for Ankole, November 1901', ESA A/15/2/82.

and sumptuous dinners and well-laden breakfast tables rise in the imagination."[166]

With such variety of provision, the trade that Macallister hoped for was certainly very soon initiated and, surprisingly quickly, so very well established. But there was another side to shopping which Major Jack goes on to discuss:

> The last part of Mbarara to be examined is the one street of shops (*dukas*, as they are always called). On either side of the street is a line of unkempt-looking shanties of wood and corrugated iron, with perhaps an occasional mud building of greater pretensions. Each shanty has a frontal verandah, on which the Indian owner [from later remarks he must mean manager] sits as a rule, and where he displays his wares. These consist of the thinnest and cheapest calicoes of every colour under the sun, and stamped with the most lurid patterns; of shoddy blankets, red fezes, beads and trinkets and tin-ware, umbrellas and so forth.[167]

He questions the commercial viability of all this merchandise on sale at such small prices.

> One marvels what the original cost of an umbrella can be, that is made perhaps in India, comes across the sea, travels up from the coast by rail, and is then transported 150 miles on a porter's head, and at the end sells for Rs. 2 and doubtless gives a handsome profit to the vendor! And the wonder is that the thing really does go up, and keeps some of the rain off.[168]

In 1970 the lines of demarcation were still there, becoming blurred, of course, but still discernible. There was a marked distinction between the high-class emporium of Aziz Virani and Jeta's supermarket nestling close to the banks (then Grindlays and our own at Barclays, DCO [Dominion, Colonial and Overseas]), and the long row of shops trailing along towards the Agip Motel in the direction of Masaka. Outside each of those would be displayed such things as a bag of posho, a

---

[166] Jack, *op. cit.*, pp.63–64. For its time, this account compares favourably with our experience in 1972. During shortages in Mbarara, we were astonished one day to find Arbroath Smokies and 'Colonel William's' frozen chickens in Jeta's supermarket

[167] *Ibid*, pp. 62–63.

[168] *Ibid*, p. 63 for this and the following two quotations.

roll of Jinja cloth.[169] In that scene there was something of a vestige of the Mbarara of Jack's day sixty odd years earlier: "Most of the *dukas* cater only for the native, and besides selling him stuff, do a good trade in hides. But some of the better class supply the Europeans as well."

> Among these are to be found certain familiar names. The ubiquitous Allidina Visram is always there. This man, said to be the biggest ivory merchant in the country, perhaps in the world, has a branch in every corner of the Protectorate.
> ... Then there are always some Goanese names, such as Souza, Figueiredo, Lobo, etc.[170]

His conclusion is that "shopping is always a delight to 99 per cent of the human race, and in these outlandish parts it is a great pleasure to go into the *dukas* and see what they have got", an experience which we later shared.[171] After another half a dozen years the official guide described "a small bazaar quarter tenanted by one Goanese merchant and some two dozen Asiatics of miscellaneous origin."[172]

Jack has also shed light on other aspects of trade. We have seen him noting porters waiting in the *boma* compound to start on a journey to Kampala, and he gives more detail still:

---

[169]   There is nothing dismissive in my description here. We used to joke that many things were easier to obtain in up-country Mbarara than in our local market town in Fife. This would have had greater emphasis when we returned to a Britain of the "Three Day Week" and candles on the counters of the shops here, had it not been for the disastrous collapse of trade in Uganda resulting from Amin's expulsion of the Asians in the previous year (1972), when we also became dependent on the ministrations of such curiosities as the 'water cart.'

[170]   Jack, *ibid*, p. 63 for this and the next quote.

[171]   "Outlandish parts" is a good description of what one finds strange and unfamiliar, especially when overseas. We first flew to Uganda just as the first men were landing on the Moon, and saw the photographs in the papers when we reached Kampala from Entebbe. A few days later we were taken by taxi to Mbarara. The further we left the capital behind, the more we wondered where we were being taken. So much of the countryside was burnt black after the firing of the grass in the dry season (it was July). We had never experienced anything like it, and it made us feel that we, too, had landed amid desolation equal to that on the moon.

[172]   See note 98 for Handbook, *op. cit.* p. 52.

This long row of melancholy-looking black scarecrows, seated squatting on the ground and clothed in scanty bits of white cloth ... are having their names taken and written on the way-bill, and they will shortly receive a rupee each as advance pay to enable them to feed themselves on the journey.[173]

This mention of rupees raises questions about how trade was carried on in this early market place which had now been set up in Mbarara. Language, currency and barter must all be now considered. In Chapter Nine language is more fully discussed, but not with any specific regard to trade. The 'Arab' and Indian traders presumably used whatever method they had applied elsewhere 'up-country.' Their speaking of *Swahili*, will initially have had little relevance except among European officials and Sudanese soldiers. They will have known some *Luganda*, too, Kampala being the centre through which they will have come. Moreover, much of such basic trade will have been able to be conducted in a fairly limited vocabulary in whatever language was used.

Traditionally currency was unknown, so that trade was carried on by barter in such commodities as the following:

crude salt, (which was traditionally extracted from Lake Katwe in south west Uganda), crude iron implements, cows, goats, cocks and bark cloth. ... Around 1825 to 1837 Ivory discs called *Sanga* became a medium of exchange. The first Arab traders came to Uganda in 1844 and they brought Cowry shells (called *Nsinda* or *Nsimbi*) with them from the coast as a medium of exchange.[174]

---

[173] Jack, *op. cit.,* p. 55.

[174] Bank of Uganda web-site (2014). There is no mention of slaves, though there were certainly some in traditional Nkore, but it is doubtful that the country was engaged in what is generally regarded as the slave trade. Major Casati only passed through with Stanley and may be a poor witness. Nevertheless his evidence is consistent with Ntare's aversion to other races entering his country. Casati states that the *omugabe* would not allow Arabs to enter, and only traded with them in ivory in exchange for guns on his borders, *op. cit.*, Vo.II p.273. That does not mean that slaves might not sometimes have been taken from such distant parts, or that no occasional caravans passed through them, see above note 46.

'A SLAVE CARAVAN'

Now Jack has mentioned rupees being used by porters on a journey, and introduced the concept of currency. As in many countries then and now, a variety of coinage was acceptable as long as it can be banked. The best example of this is the Maria Theresa Dollar (*Thaler*), a large heavy silver coin, much used along the East African coast, and in some parts of the world still. It originated in 1741 but usually bears the date 1780. That coastal region then became part of the Rupee zone, rather than Sterling, partly because of the use of Indian workers. In 1889, the I.B.E.A.Co. had its own rupees and pice minted to replace cowries. There were also Zanzibari pice (*pysa*) first minted in Birmingham in 1882. With the traders operating throughout East Africa, all of these would have had value. Coins were introduced for East Africa, and then in 1906–07 the first for the 'East Africa and Uganda Protectorates' were minted. These were in shillings divided into one hundred cents, and twenty shillings equalling a pound Sterling.

So here we have the background to the use of currency in local trading for which several types of coinage will have been acceptable. It seems likely that the local custom of bartering will have been used for the trade in skins. A merchant could well afford to part with goods in exchange for such commodities. They could be sold on at a profit. Though not mentioned, if it was available ivory may have been similarly exchanged, or equally bought for cash.

At Independence, Uganda wisely stuck to its Shilling and it was almost a decade before the Imperial currency ceased to have cash value. Yet the introduction of currency to a society that has known only barter may sound straight forward enough, but it has its own complexities even under an independent Uganda currency. Over four decades ago a highly intelligent, university educated Ugandan District Official surprised the writer by saying that he would never get used to a moneyed economy. Having been brought up in a rural area dependent only on exchange, it would always be a foreign concept to him.

CHAPTER EIGHT

CHRISTIAN MISSIONS

At the same time missionary activities were also developing. By December 1898 neither Anglicans nor Catholics were carrying on missionary work in Nkore. The first real Christian penetration had come when the *Baganda* Christians sought succour there in 1888–90. As refugees they had not been in a position to do much to proclaim their faith,[175] but some, like Apolo Kaggwa and Zakaria Kizito, made a considerable impression at Ntare's court. They were settled in Kabula, near the Buganda border, and where Mbaguta was the chief; he was strongly impressed, become the blood-brother of two of the leading Christians, and as has already been seen from Bishop Tucker's account, permanently adopted *Kiganda* ways. Certainly his influence was crucial in the later acceptance of Christianity at the court. As time went on, the situation for someone like him must have been particularly confusing.[176] So at the end of the century Mbaguta was rather inconsistent towards the new influences despite these Christian contacts.

Thus when the *Kabaka* Mwanga rebelled in 1897 he fought on that side with Kintu's army, but then Kintu had also once been a Christian refugee in Nkore, and even after his final escape to German territory he still claimed to be a Catholic.[177] The real irony of the situation however is seen in the fact that it was Mbaguta's force fighting for Kintu at Nyendo Hill in that August which led to the European determination to control 'Ankole' and which was to be so much to the former's ad-

---

[175] Wright, *op. cit.*, pp. 69–74; Stanley met with some of them in 1889, *op. cit.* (1890) pp. 350–352.

[176] See Karugire, *op. cit.* (1973).

[177] Wright, *op. cit.* p. 194.

vantage. Following the battle George Wilson wrote that,

> After grave deliberation upon the conditions surrounding
> the whole position I have ventured to assume that Ankoli's
> attitude has afforded sufficient justification for the conse-
> quences, which may accrue to that country from Mr.
> Grant's incursion.[178]

One of the consequences was the conviction of the Commissioner, Berkeley, that it was essential to settle the country
through administration, and in the wake of this the Missions
became established also.

Mbaguta is bound to be in for a thin time from certain
quarters, for having embraced the 'progressive' *Baganda* and
European ways, and for later having encouraged Christianity,
education and the Protectorate administration along with his
own advancement. Critics often forget that he helped to cata-
pult Ankole into the twentieth century. It is a little odd, therefore to find a highly educated *Munyankore* historian[179] on the
staff of the History Department of Makerere saying that

> Mbaguta was no more 'progressive' than all his other rivals
> who refused to co-operate with them because his very posi-
> tion depended on the goodwill of the colonial officials of
> the period.[180]

Elsewhere he says,

> He was 'progressive', which term in colonial parlance,
> means that he collaborated with the colonial administration
> in enforcing some of the policies which did not appeal ei-
> ther to the king or even to the people.[181]

Does 'progressive' really mean no more than this? In the wid-
est context this characteristic is seen in Mbaguta's willingness
to accept change and embrace new ideas, which is evident
even *before* the arrival of the colonialists. Undoubtedly there
was much opposition to the 'progressive' ideas, but to discuss
them with such scepticism would be more acceptable from a
Muhima who still lives a pastoral life in Nyabushozi. It is dif-

---

[178]   *Africa* (no. 2), 1898, *op. cit.*, Wilson to the Marquess of Salisbury, 15
        September 1897.

[179]   See also below, note 215.

[180]   Karugire, (1971), *op. cit.*, p. 248.

[181]   *Ibid*, p. 111.

ficult to avoid the conclusion that this view is only an expression of the party line of a particular group of non-African scholars, who are unable to think of human actions being motivated by anything except political considerations.[182]

Of course, there were other progressives among the *Banyankore* and even the *Bahinda,* despite Karugire's blanket assertion and compelling case that the ruling clan had an overwhelming "incurable and somewhat unreasonable dislike of having Europeans in the kingdom."[183]. We can take the example of Bucunku. There was already his *omukago* relationship with the Europeans through Stanley, and also considerable warmth towards the new faith which they had brought (he was later baptized as Apolo), and such factors should be taken seriously. In October 1902 he dictated in *Runyankore* a letter to his "friend" Stanley which Willis first wrote down and then also put into English for him. We have no reason to doubt that the words expressed the feelings he sought to convey, and he also affirms the offer of the main obligation of *omukago,* that of helping the other:

> I rejoice very much in my heart to write. ... If you shall be wanting anything, send to me, and I shall send it to you. Now I am reading the Gospel. ... Our King Kahaya, and many men, are reading to be baptized. ... God is wonderful, to bring me ... and you to this (time) ... – to know one another ... to make His word reach to us, and to make us know the name of Jesus Christ.[184]

Again, it is instructive to read a second generation view. Kezekiya Katukula had no formal education, became a Chris-

---

[182] See E. I. Steinhart, 'Primary collaboration in Ankole 1891-1901 — an interpretation of the response to the colonial impact', Makerere U.E.A., S.S.C., History Papers, pp. 195–196 and footnote 31 on p. 197. Karugire says that among the *Bahima* there was little interest in education until the 1950s, *op. cit.* (1973) p. 46. This is born out by the writer's experience of friendship with *Bahima* officials in local government two decades later. Some had brothers who were still maintaining the traditional way of life among their cattle in the grasslands.

[183] Karugire, *op .cit.* (1973) p. 46. This blanket judgment is too strong.

[184] *UJ* 30 (1966) pp. 209–210.

tian, learnt to read and write, and rose to become a *Saza* Chief in the 1940s and 50s. His eldest son, James Kahigiriza, was born in 1921, did have formal education at Mbarara High School and Budo, rising even higher to become the last *Enganzi* before the Kingdom was abolished in 1967. Looking back over a long life, this was his view:

> Compared to most of my contemporaries, I was lucky to be born and brought up in a progressive family. My father's uncle recognized the importance of literacy brought about by Christianity and colonial education and was therefore keen to spread the art of reading and writing in the family and the community at large. Accordingly my father was one of the first beneficiaries of the spread of literacy in colonial Ankole. He learnt how to read from the Native Anglican Church.[185]

Therefore, it is more than possible that H. F. Morris was right (and it would seem to be far more true of human nature) to say, "Imperious and ambitious though he no doubt was, Mbaguta had also a sincere belief in progress,"[186] and especially in those particular facets of progress already mentioned. Moreover, those engaged in primary opposition to European involvement as reactionaries were seeking to maintain a traditional way of life which was under threat from other quarters and which Karugire did not believe could have survived.[187]

The leading *Baganda* Christians of the exile retained their concern that the Gospel should be brought to Nkore, but while Ntare V lived, little could be done directly. The very earliest attempt would seem to have been by two *Baganda* teachers

---

[185]   Kahigiriza, J. *Bridging the Gap*, Kampala (2001) p. 3. In an intriguing twist he tells us that "his father's uncle" was "the prime minister to Musinga wa Karetwa, the last king of Igara kingdom", *ibid*, who was anything but progressive, see note 14.

[186]   *UJ*, 24, 1960, p. 1.

[187]   Karugire, *op. cit.* (1971), p. 250, and he implies it again in (1973) p. 25 where he graphically describes the threats to the *Banyankore* from rinderpest which crippled the herds of the pastoralists; smallpox and jiggers could affect anyone in the population; as might the depredations caused by fierce attacks from the *Banyarwanda*. It is no wonder that Europeans thought the *Bahima* to be a dying race, Macallister to Ternan, 10 July 1899, ESA A/4/19/469.

THE REVEREND HERBERT
CLAYTON of the C. M. S.

who were working in Nkore before the end of August 1894, though one wonders how far they had penetrated, and nothing seems to have resulted.[188] Among the European missionaries there was also a real concern.

Too often Bishop Willis is credited with having pioneered the Protestant advance into Ankole.[189] In fact he only reached Uganda in December 1900, and came to Mbarara in the following month with Herbert Clayton, who was the real European pioneer. Willis was only there until 1902, whereas Clayton was in Ankole much of the time until 1912.[190]

The C.M.S. lay missionary, George Pilkington had a great

---

[188] Pirouet, M. M. L. Ph.D. University of East Africa, 1968 (later published as *Black Evangelists: the Spread of Christianity in Uganda 1891–1914,* London (1978); see 'Evangelists and sub-imperialists', *Dini na Mila, Vol.* 4, no. 1, October 1969, pp. 28–41. For the parts played by Clayton and Willis, see Weekes, D. *op. cit.* (forthcoming).

[189] Notably in C.M.S. publications, see for instance, Stock, E., *History of the C.M.S.,* Vol. 4, London (1916), and Gresford Jones, H., *Uganda in transformation,* London (1926), p. 160. The eclipse of the role of the true Protestant pioneer seems now complete, with a principal street in Mbarara called 'Bishop Willis' rather than 'Herbert Clayton Road'. Willis only left the country after serving as Bishop from 1912 to 1934, but had no close daily contact in Ankole after 1902; but see next.

[190] What is said in the previous note should be balanced by the grass-roots view which Dr Kagume discovered from his oral informants, and very properly included: "Clayton earned a high reputation among the *Banyankore,* and he was very much liked. As a comment on his punctuality and enthusiasm [they] nicknamed him *Rutakyerererwe rwa Katonya* (he who ever gets there on time)." *op. cit.,* (1973) p. 52. That translation is similar to the one the writer was given over forty years ago "Keretoni, the one who is never late, the son of Katoonya".

desire to see the Gospel taken to more out-lying areas, and early in 1896, soon after Ntare's death, he wrote 'A Three Year Enterprise for Uganda' in which he mentioned 'Ankole' as one of those places that "are within reach and touch, though not absolutely open at present."[191] One of his boys, Aloni Muhinda, had his origins in Nkore and would later become the first *Munyankole* to be ordained deacon in the Protestant Church. Clayton, who arrived in Uganda early in 1897 with the same party as Dr Cook, was sent to work in Koki with R. H. Leakey.[192] In June 1897 Pilkington visited Koki and addressed some meetings. Clayton wrote that

> some of the missionaries are very anxious to get an entrance into Ankole and to send teachers there, but so far it has not been considered safe for a European to go there. We have however just sent one of our teachers in to see the King of Ankole and to find out if he would receive teachers.[193]

The moment of course proved to be extremely inopportune as a week later the *Kabaka* Mwanga fled from Mengo. Sometime afterwards Leakey reported on this:

> Just before the rebellion broke out we sent one of our teachers from here to visit Kahaya, the King of Ankole, and to see what prospect of work there was there. Ankole has always been very anti-European and our messenger was received with great suspicion as the agent of the Europeans. Kahaya would say nothing save that he would send to Kampala [to Mwanga] to know if he should allow us to enter Ankole. Our messengers found the people deeply sunk in superstition. Some were more or less anxious to hear what we had to say, but were afraid of their friends. [194]

The first real attempt to place two native evangelists at

---

[191]   Pilkington, G. 'A three year enterprise for Uganda', *Church Missionary Intelligencer,* May 1896, p. 335.

[192]   Leakey, always known as Harry, was at that time still a layman. The family have on-going fame in East Africa through this Canon Leakey's son, Louis, and grandson, Richard. A daughter was married to the first Archbishop of East Africa, Dr Beecher.

[193]   C. L., 8th July 1897. The name of this man was Firipo Muwanga, the head teacher in Koki. Clayton, Letters; 4th September 1904.

[194]   Leakey, R. *Church Missionary Intelligencer,* (1898), p. 416.

Kahaya's court came at the end of 1898 from the former refugee, Kaggwa; but the opposition proved too strong, and they returned to Buganda. Canon Buningwire gives their names as Timeseo and Nuwa.[195]

The second attempt was made in May 1899, just before Kahaya moved in to Kamukuzi. Herbert Clayton "who had long had his eyes fixed upon Nkole" took the opportunity of the initiative of the *Mugema*[196] (Yoswa Kate Damulira) in getting permission from the Church Council at Namirembe to send two of his own followers as teachers into Ankole and to go there himself. His letters describe this visit to Rushasha and the short stop at "the Fort, where Mr. Macallister ... gave me tea with bread and jam." He arrived on 23rd May, and on the next day he recorded only the *Omugabe*'s refusal to agree to the evangelists remaining in his territory. The strangers were given hospitality by Mbaguta who "says he would be glad to read, only he is afraid of the King and the old heathen his chief advisers."

At first Clayton found that "the King is very much under the influence of an old chief named Igumira, who was I believe his guardian and who is a determined heathen and opposed to any change."[197] However Kahaya's new independence of the old chiefs, already seen in his decision to move to Mbarara also made at this time, is now seen in his change of attitude towards these Christians. Clayton does not elaborate on what caused the change – if he ever knew – but by 29th May he could write that "Kahaya has reconsidered his decision and has consented to receive our teacher and allow his people to be taught."[198] It was a very small beginning, with only five men reading, while Kahaya and the chiefs played a waiting game to

---

[195] Personal communication from Canon Yoeri Buningwire, 11th November 1969.

[196] Hereditary *Saza* Chief of Busiro in the kingdom of Buganda and Head of the Monkey Clan.

[197] C. L., 24th and 25th May 1899; see also Tucker, A. R. *Eighteen Years in Uganda and East Africa*, London (1908), Vol. 2, pp. 232 and 236–237.

[198] C. L., 29th May 1899.

see what would befall them. Clayton then returned to Koki leaving the evangelists at Rushasha for it appears that there were two, Sitefano Kagumisa and Yokana Nakaima, while one of Clayton's 'boys', Isaka Nyakayaga, was also of the party.[199] Once again the opposition proved too strong, and the teachers returned.

The real beginning of Protestant missionary work in Mbarara can be dated from December 1899. In August, Zakaria Kizito, now the *Kangawo*,[200] visited Mbarara and later told Clayton "that the King Kahaya is now anxious for a European teacher to go and live there" and the suggestion was made that Clayton should go and build there, again leaving *Baganda* teachers in charge until a European could be freed to go there.[201] This was not taken up, but the way was prepared for Bishop Tucker and Dr Cook, when they passed through Ankole "if possible to effect an entrance" on their way to Toro in December 1899. Stopping in Koki on the way they discussed the prospects with Clayton, who was able to introduce them to Filipo Bamulanzeki and Andereya Kamya who "were prepared as missionaries to give themselves to the work of teaching the *Banyankole* the truths of Christianity."[202] Again there was some difficulty in getting the two men accepted, but Tucker and Cook were able to leave them behind and these two stayed.

Four months later, Clayton in Buddu had good news of their progress. They reported to him

> that the king, Kahaya, has made a start in learning to read, but that he is not keen about it, and many of his big chiefs wish to prevent him. The *Katikiro*, or Prime Minister, Baguta is much keener about it, and is anxious that all his women and boys should learn. He wants very much some European missionary to go and spend at least a fortnight with them, when he thinks that the king would really make

---

199 See note 197; Taylor, *op. cit.* p. 65; Nyakayaga is the same man later tried and exiled because of the murder of Galt.

200 *Saza* Chief of Bulemezi in the kingdom of Buganda.

201 C. L., 3rd September 1899.

202 Tucker, A. R. *op. cit.* pp. 232 and 236–237.

a start in earnest.[203]

Clayton went to visit the new Mission in September 1900, a month after Macallister had left for the Nile, and found that "Kahaya is building a small Church close to his own fence" and "Mbaguta is our keenest reader."[204]

The first reference to Mission activity in the official correspondence reflects similar attempts by the Roman Catholics to enter Ankole. There had of course been many among the Christians of the exile, and the Catholic leader, Honorato Nyonyintono, had become a blood-brother of Ntare's son. In establishing permanent work in Ankole they experienced the same difficulties as the Protestants. Then in May 1899 Macallister told Ternan that "the native sent by Monsieur Gorju [Superior of the White Fathers, Bikira] went to Kawia and came back rather disgusted. He reports having failed to find a single man willing to be taught."[205] A few weeks later there is an interesting sidelight on Clayton's very first visit and the (temporary) establishing of the *Mugema's* two men:

> A Mr. Clayton of the C.M.S. called here on his way to Kawia on May 23rd, and again on his way back to Koki on May 31st. He informs me that two teachers were sent away from Kawia's a short time ago, this may be correct as I told Kawia not to allow any *Waganda* to remain in Ankole without a pass, it being impossible to distinguish between *Waangoni* and other *Waganda*, Kawia now allows two teachers to live near him, and has given them each a slave to teach."[206]

It rounds off the story to add that from January 1901 the Reverends Herbert Clayton and J. J. Willis, of the Church Missionary Society, took over the direction of the work[207] begun

---

[203]   Tucker, A. R. *op. cit.;* Clayton, Letter from Kajuna, 24th April 1900 quoted in *Church Missionary Intelligencer,* (1900), p. 611.

[204]   C. L., 21st September 1900.

[205]   Macallister to Ternan, 8th May 1899, ESA A/4/16/188.

[206]   Macallister to Ternan, 2nd June 1899, ESA A/4/17/264a. The need for a pass seems to have been overlooked by other writers such as Lukyn Williams (1935, 2/3), Bamunoba (1966/67), *ops. cit.*

[207]   A personal anecdote can illustrate the warmth with which the C.M.S. missionaries in Ankole were remembered years later. I arrived in

by the two Koki teachers at Kamukuzi and thereafter rapid development took place. Monseigneur Streicher was very keen on extending from Buddu and Koki into Ankole and Père Gorju seems to have been the counterpart of Clayton. As director of the White Fathers work in Koki he was to become the leader of the first permanent Catholic centre at Mbarara. A determined attempt was made from Koki in the last months of 1900 by Père J. Lesbros, Brother Herman and the *Munyankole* catechist Jean Kamondo, who conducted a fact-finding tour. Kamondo was left behind to build a church, but the venture ran into political difficulties. The work did not properly begin until the arrival of Père Gorju and Père Varangot in October 1902 when the Mission at Nyamitanga was started.

Muslim activity at Mbarara was slight. Though Muslims had come to Ankole several years before, they had found little response among the local people. At this time they were mainly represented by the soldiers of the Uganda Rifles.[208]

Mbarara in Government employment and as an Associate Missionary of the C.M.S. after an interval in which there had been no white clergyman living and working within the diocese of Ankole. Sometimes, pupils at Ntare would ask me to go out to village churches to preach while they interpreted. Greeting worshippers afterwards I was frequently asked, "Are you C.M.S.?" Happily able to answer in the affirmative, faces would light up and become wreathed in smiles at my response. Similarly, when the CMS General Secretary, John Taylor, visited in about 1970, he addressed a large gathering of the diocese. Suggesting that from now on the C.M.S. should only send an annual cheque, he was greeted with cries of "No, send us people!"

[208]   Commissioner to Galt, 6th October 1902, *ESA* A/15/1/33 of 1902 (the arrival of Catholic fathers.) Soldiers in Mbarara are often referred to as 'Sudanese'. Any doubt about the religion is disposed of in the correspondence between Bishop Streicher and the Commissioner after the withdrawal of Père Lesbros from Ankole because of political involvements. The Bishop, Kisubi, 11th October 1901 "je renonce pour cette année a l'établissement de la station qui j'avais dessein d'y fonder prochainement pour le service religieux des soldats *Baganda* presque tous catholiques, qui composent la garnison due Fort de Mbarara." The Mbarara Police Force, started a year before, was however made up mainly of *Baganda* and *Bakoki,* quite a number of whom were Protestant Christians, and doubtless others were Catholics. (C.L. 21st Sept. 1900). To this, Jackson, Acting Commissioner, replied on the following day: "Ankole is at present garrisoned by No. 6 and

For interest sake, we can conclude with Major Jack's comments about the two Christian Missions several years later. Of the Protestants (C.M.S.) he says that they have built a Church "a good-sized edifice of brick." There is the house where the missionary lives with his family, and "a native boys' school" about which he has this to say: "the schoolboys wear a sort of uniform ... the long white *kanzu* and a cap bearing a school or mission badge. They look very neat and their manners struck me as being excellent."[209]

He is rather more doubtful about another initiative in the form of "a school for small girls, which was just being started by Miss Baker." Perhaps because he discovered that her father and brother belonged to the same Regiment as himself, he was sufficiently interested to go and see

> The provision that had been made for the future pupils in the shape of a schoolroom and dormitory. The difficulties that confront Miss Baker in her self-imposed task are considerably greater that would at first be imagined.

There is a lack of understanding in his awareness in then speaking of only one tribe in the area.

> This is a country of the *Bahima*, and the only training a *Muhima* girl receives is to sit still all day and suck milk through a straw, growing fat and conforming to the *Muhima* ideal of female beauty. To let their daughter go and be trained by the white man means to the *Bahima* that they will be not only ugly but probably useless.

While "one cannot but sympathise with the desire to raise these girls from the somewhat cow-like condition to which they are doomed" his conclusion is not optimistic. "Whether it will conduce to their ultimate happiness is quite another question." Certainly there were those for whom that would be true.

Like some other European visitors, Jack was clearly very

No. 10 Companies, Uganda Rifles, which companies are composed solely of Sudanese." No. 6 Coy had been stationed at Mbarara ever since Macallister's arrival. (ESA A/24/1/8 & 10 of 1901). See also below, note 273.

[209] The quotations in this paragraph are taken from Jack, *op. cit.* p. 61. The *kanzu,* of course, was not a local garment, but a recent acquisition through the traders.

impressed when visiting the Mission station of the White Fathers, already established across the Ruizi at Nyamitanga. Again, there was much there with a military air about it which would appeal to a professional soldier like the writer:

> One's first impression … is that of rich *shambas*; of trim, well kept gardens, and walks; and of an air of monasticism. The French Fathers are celibates; their building takes the form of a quadrangle; the living rooms and dormitories surrounding a fruit and vegetable garden. … These men when they come to the country do so for life, unless an absolute breakdown in health necessitates their return. They appear to live entirely on what the country produces, with the possible exception of an occasional glass of light wine. … It is impossible not to admire the devotion to their faith which causes men to cut themselves off so utterly from all home ties. They are a fine, manly set of fellows who inspire respect.[210]

Nuwa Mbaguta by Dr Karugire[211]

The names of many Europeans are scattered throughout this present book and some are listed in Appendix A. The lives of notable members of the indigenous population are probably best investigated by others like themselves. In the year after this Chapter was written, Dr Karugire published a small book on *Nuwa Mbaguta*, much to be welcomed.[212]

It is clear that the author has an ambivalent attitude towards his subject. He has great sympathy with the traditionalists centred around Igumira, who resisted, or rather sought to ignore, the fledging British administration in Ankole. At the same time he seeks to be fair, and concludes that "Mbaguta was a great man for collaborators are not necessarily bad men

---

[210]   Jack, *op. cit.* p. 62.

[211]   See also above note 182.

[212]   Karugire, S. R. *Nuwa Mbaguta and the Establishment of British Rule in Ankole,* Nairobi, (1973) in a series entitled 'Uganda's Famous Men.' It is reviewed in *UJ,* **80**, 1982, pp. 60–62. There is also Lukyn Williams, F., 'Nuwa Mbaguta, Nganzi of Ankole', *UJ,* **10/2**, 1946, pp. 127–129.

on account of being collaborators."[213] He also recognises that "there were mixed motives on both sides, whether they were consciously perceived or not."[214]

The writer has every sympathy with this equivocal attitude towards one's country's past, being sometimes saddened by the loss of a traditional British way of life, aspects of which he remembers from long ago; but it is easy to romanticise and forget the negatives, for without the 'progressives' he would not be typing this upon his laptop.

Dr Karugire had been a pupil at Ntare School in Mbarara a few years before I was Church of Uganda Chaplain there between 1969-1973. Sometimes I have wondered what it would be like for a British boy to grow up, perhaps under Japanese rule, having to learn that language for all school purposes and to find that all text books, as well as virtually everything in the school library was in that alien tongue. Thus it is not surprising that there is a certain ambiguity in Dr Karugire's views. He observes that Mbaguta's "interest in education, such as it was, was genuine."[215] That kind of education was one of the fruits of collaboration, and the young Karugire had advanced through his secondary schooling based on the British Independent boarding system, under a Scottish Headmaster, to a University which owed its inception to the work of C.M.S. missionaries. He studied for his doctorate in London, and was clearly rightly proud that his thesis on Ankole history had been published by the Oxford University Press. Had primary opposition to the introduction of British administration in Ankole succeeded, it is unlikely that any of this would have been possible.

It must also be acknowledged that his own oral information was obtained some forty years after the researches by Lukyn Williams and a score or so after H. F. Morris, both of whose findings he criticises, though not without some cause. Occasionally his prejudice overflows, as when he attempts to

---

[213] *Ibid*, pp. 86–87.

[214] *Ibid*, p. 6.

[215] *Ibid*, p. 4.

rename the First World War as "the European Civil War."[216]

Despite modestly acknowledging that he can only hope to throw "some light, no matter how dim" on the process of "British occupation and the role of local collaboration"[217] in Ankole, Dr Karugire makes a convincing case for our better understanding of Mbaguta. However, he does not touch on one aspect of his experience which may well have motivated his progressive attitudes. We have seen that in the previous decade Mbaguta was much influenced by the *Baganda* exiles over whom he was placed when they came into Nkore for sanctuary. Many of these were Christians. In addition he had a good knowledge of Buganda and had worked with the Catholic 'rebel' Kintu. It seems untenable for Karugire to say that Mbaguta could not "have known who Catholics were in 1900."[218] That was the year after Christian missionaries settled into Ankole in the wake of the arrival of a British administrator.

Mbaguta gave much encouragement and became an early C.M.S. convert. The profound effect of such an acceptance of Christianity upon a person's life and attitudes should never be underestimated. It will explain much about Mbaguta's continuing support for progressive ways as against a dogged maintenance of the traditional life. Moreover, Mbaguta's great kindness and generosity which is stressed by Dr Karugire,[219] may also be attributed to the inspiration of this source.

Samwiri Rubaraza Karugire served as Head of the History Department at the University of Zambia, Deputy Foreign Affairs Minister in the post-Amin UNLF Government and as Professor and Head of History Department at Makerere Universi-

---

216   *Ibid*, p. 52; but the First World War, (which prefaced a Second that was equally widespread) was indeed worldwide, involved nations that were in no way European, and even its origins were not wholly in that continent. It was a moving experience to attend Remembrance Day parades in Mbarara where veterans, clad in their bits of uniform some with medals, and with shouldered wooden staffs in lieu of rifles, marched proudly past – and remembered.

217   Karugire, *op. cit.* (1973), p. 6.

218   *Ibid*, p. 45.

219   *Ibid*, pp.71–73.

ty. From the beginning of 1987 he was Director General of the Customs & Excise Department of the Ministry of Finance.[220]

His tragically premature death in 1992 is greatly to be lamented. He was a distinguished Ugandan historian, and I am sorry that our paths failed to cross at Ntare, and in the early 1970s when we were both engaged on research into Ankole history. One can greatly respect a scholar for the quality of his research and writing while disagreeing with some of his conclusions. I was fortunate to meet both the earlier local historians, Messrs Kamugungunu and Katate, and Yoramu Bamunoba, Chaplain of Bishop Stuart College (and since Bishop), was a good friend and colleague. Not everyone will agree with my interpretations but they are genuinely held and sincerely expressed, just as no doubt were theirs. It would have been an added privilege to have met him, too.

Dr Kagume's Thesis[221]

This very interesting and well written account is of only marginal concern to us here. He has a few pages on 'Religious Beliefs' (16–21), a few on 'British Contact and Colonisation' (31–37), with rather more on the first two decades of the coming of Christianity to Nkore (45–73). Although his writing is very convincing, caution is needed over accepting some of his conclusions. This may be partly because his interest is more concerned with sociology than with history. Three examples can be given.

As a result of the conflicts within Buganda which were partly engendered by religious differences, he believes that the C.M.S. lost its nerve over expansion outside Buganda unless it was under the protection of the new Imperial power:

> the practical consequence of this loss of confidence was that after the introduction of the British administration in Uganda, the CMS Mission was content to follow the trail of

---

[220] Website for African Books Directive.

[221] Kagume, A. M. 'Church and Society in Ankole, Uganda: An Analysis of the Impact of Evangelical Anglican Christianity on Ethnic and Gender Relations in Ankole, 1901–1961.' PhD. University of Bristol (1993).

the colonial administration.[222]

This is hardly fair to the C.M.S. Much in history is co-incidental rather than deliberately planned and the C.M.S. failure to enter Nkore before the Administration was not from want of trying.

Moreover, Kagume has acknowledged the years of courageous pioneering in Buganda without the support of British rule. Elsewhere, missionaries could not just walk into the surrounding territory and start evangelising. Moreover, he rightly recognises three inhibiting factors preventing such enterprise when the Protectorate was set up in 1894, (although not even potentially extended to include Nkore until 1896).

(1) The C.M.S. was excluded because they and the White Father's had been persuaded to restrict themselves to separate areas of influence, the C.M.S. in the north and east of the country, the Fathers in the south and west (including Nkore).

(2) Its missionaries were excluded because the rulers of Nkore (initially in the person of Ntare) were not then in favour of European influence or intervention by either missions or administration.

(3) Even without these two obstacles they might still have been deterred because it was known that the food supply was likely to prove very difficult for any strangers who went there.

None of these restrictions prevented Pilkington and Clayton from setting their eyes on possibilities in Nkore as early as 1897, or deterred the Bugandan Church from sending evangelists even before that.[223] All this we have seen.

There would be a fourth inhibition. The unsettled state of

---

[222] *Ibid*, p. 48.

[223] The indigenous Buganda Church was not bound by the agreement between the Missions. That proved very temporary anyway, since The Fathers responded by getting into the C.M.S. areas of the north and east by asking a British Order of Catholics, the Mill Hill Fathers to commence work there. This began in 1898. Thereafter the C.M.S. were free to work in the south and west, including Nkore. Kagume says that Fathers had not yet entered Ankole because "they were preoccupied with planning how to encroach on the CMS' eastern territory" *op. cit.* pp. 51–52, but, as Europeans, they were actually kept away by the same inhibitions as the C.M.S.

the country arising from Mwanga's flight from Kampala, and the Sudanese Mutiny made such advance impossible. Therefore, altogether it seems unjustified to charge the C.M.S. with a rather cowardly approach. Apart from shortage of manpower, Pilkington and Clayton could do nothing from Koki before 1898 because of the four reasons given above, and by then the former had been killed in courageous circumstances, see p. 96.

As it turned out, it is true that the C.M.S. did not successfully penetrate Ankole until after the Administration had been extended there. It was only thereafter that permission for mission was obtained from the rulers. By then the taboo against a meeting between the *Omugabe* and a European had been broken. This was a necessary prerequisite, and as it happened it had occurred for political reasons not for religious ones. There may be something in Dr Kagume's view, but it tends to be an *a posteriori* argument and not the whole story.

It is curious therefore that he should emphasise the fact that when Clayton and Willis first arrived to take up permanent residence, they went first to Kahaya's *orurembo* at Rushasha, and only after that to the Administrative headquarters at Mbarara.[224] If they were really so afraid and dependent upon Imperial protection their route should have been reversed!

Secondly, he completely plays down the aversion of the *Omugabe* to meeting with a European, saying that the reason for this is unknown. He rightly dismisses Lugard's assertion that Ntare was too fat to walk, but that misunderstanding probably arose from reports that the leading *Banyankore* were carried about in baskets, which was true (see photograph herein of Igumira in such conveyance). The two earlier *Banyankore* historians are quite clear about the great difficulty of "showing" Kahaya to a European, as discussed above, and the ensuing problems. Nevertheless, he ably brings out more clearly than others the nature of the food problem, showing that it was difficult for *Bahima* pastoralists to feed *Baganda* evangelists who ate vegetables, coupled with the cultural difficulty of *Bahima* sharing their milk with others.

Thirdly, he then claims that when the C.M.S. did come

---

[224]   Kagume, *op. cit.* p. 59.

they ignored the *Bairu* and only seemed to recognize the existence of the *Bahima* among whom they worked. On his own admission this ignorance only lasted a short time. He quotes the "Annual Letter 1903" from Willis showing his full awareness. This appeared in print in London under the date 29th October 1903. However, it was actually his letter for 1902 and must have referred to realities before he ceased to work in Ankole at the end of that year, that is less than two years since their first arrival. Moreover, Kagume is very clear that the *Bairu* tended to avoid the grasslands of the *Bahima,* and that they were largely concentrated to the north-east of the country.

Since the C.M.S. men had to deal with the *Omugabe* in order to begin any work in Ankole, it is not surprising that their initial activity was on the grasslands where the ruler was to be found, and surrounded there by *Bahima*. The White Fathers did not have this difficulty, but came in the following year on the "tail' of the Protestants who had already established acceptance of a mission presence. They always had greater manpower resources and it is no surprise that they quickly established themselves among the much larger *Bairu* population at a distance from Mbarara.

CHAPTER NINE

LANGUAGES USED IN COMMUNICATION

A discussion of communication raises some essential questions. How did the different races converse with each other? To what extent were individuals willing to learn languages other than their own? Would one of the *Bantu* ones become dominant? Could the *Runyankore* vernacular survive?

Africans, Asians and Europeans encountered one another more or less unexpectedly in the founding of Mbarara. The languages involved were the local ones, together with *Swahili*, and English (less so French and marginally German). They corresponded to the racial groups, but how did they manage to converse?[225]

Though *Swahili* is sometimes thought of as an African language, this mongrel tongue of the East Africa Coast was of little utility a thousand miles inland. English was then only of relevance to the handful of British officials who were required to learn *Swahili*, but beyond any usefulness that might have, they depended on interpreters. Thus Protectorate officials could adequately carry on their activities and "get by" through their knowledge of *Swahili*. In all other necessities they could expect to rely on translation, though some knew *Luganda*.[226]

---

[225] This matter of language is discussed more fully in Weekes, *op. cit.* (forthcoming).

[226] Administration relied heavily upon *Baganda* for translators into the vernacular of *Runyankore* (especially using Christians who had been exiles in Nkore in the early 1890s and had learnt it then) and also *Banyankore* who themselves had spent time in Buganda. This is amply demonstrated at the signing of the Ankole Agreement. written only in English, with no prior translation into *Luganda*, Wilson asked Willis to do this on the spot. Being in Uganda only a few months, he was unable to cope with legal terms; Wilson, too, tried in *Luganda* and

Moreover, their responsibilities required them to be able to communicate with the leaders of the country, rather than with the population as a whole. Whatever criticism is made of indirect rule,[227] it was certainly the method by which the wishes of the Administration were conveyed to the people. Furthermore, whether by accident or misunderstanding, rather than design, the system of government organisation in Buganda came to be introduced into Ankole. Thus at the time of the Ankole Agreement of 1901 Mbaguta was recognised as the 'Prime Minister' (*Katikiro* in Buganda; *Enganzi* in *Runyankore*) a position previous unknown according to Karugire. More and more the Administration dealt through him, and the *Omugabe* came to be marginalised.[228]

Since those days there has long been an issue about the vernacular languages used within Uganda. Should one or another be dominant in particular areas or throughout the whole land? Indeed, should any outside language be dominant? In

---

failed, yet the task was "very thoroughly done." When Racey translated English into *Swahili*, an interpreter declaimed it in *Luganda*, and finally Willis's "teacher", Isaka (Nyakayaga), having lived in Buganda, called it out in "*Luhima*" – see W.J.1/232-234, 7th August 1901. Of course the exercise can be criticised but, unlike Willis, Doronbos misrepresents it as a total farce, *op. cit.* (1975) p. 57.

227   Karugire is strong on this, though weak on argument *op. cit.* (1973), pp.43–44 and 65–66 *et al.* Imperialism had its faults, but what was the alternative? It is not well founded to criticise George Wilson for appreciating Igumira's strong points while banishing him for subversion. One can see strong qualities in Idi Amin but not be bound to approve of his actions. If Igurima was Ankole's 'first nationalist' (p. 65) as Karugire claims, one has to ask where success in that role would have led. On his own admission Nkore would probably have been overwhelmed by invasion from such enemies as the *Banyarwanda*, and by deadly diseases if left to itself in the 1890s (see above note 187). It is inconceivable that Nkore could still exist today in its age old traditional way of life in accordance with Igumira's 'nationalism'. Other predators would have gobbled it up and perhaps more viciously. Any repression by the British pales into insignificance compared with what has happened elsewhere, and since Independence. The fact that Ankole no longer exists as a political entity is the work of post-colonial government.

228   *Ibid*, pp. 84–85.

time English would become the national language of Uganda for the purposes of Government and higher education. Even in the 1970s there was much discussion as to whether it should rather now be *Swahili* which was by this time widely spoken in some other parts of East Africa. A memorable letter from a schoolboy was published in the national press saying that he would rather have the language of the imperialists than the language of the slave trade. There were other considerations in favour of English, but the difficulty has been illustrated.

The same is true of Ankole and the *Bantu* languages of the south of the country.[229] Speakers of the various tongues within this group are generally said to be able to understand what others say to them, but have difficulty in replying in a vernacular other than their own. Would it not be better in time to adopt one language, perhaps *Luganda*, for the whole?

The first missionaries to arrive were Protestants associated with the activities of the Church Missionary Society (Anglican), followed soon afterwards by the White Fathers (French Roman Catholics). The language issue then became much more complex.

Unlike the Administrators their daily concern was engaging with all levels of local society. They sought to communicate the Gospel to the indigenous people. Eventually, some British administrators like Morris, took a lively interest in *Runyankore*, the local vernacular and encouraged its use. Even earlier, men like Lukyn Williams showed a real interest in recording *Kinyankore* traditional ways. During the second half of the twentieth century scholarly interest was also aroused.

However, from the start knowledge of the vernacular was a key concern for the missionaries if they were to pass on the intimate detail of the faith. It was impossible to convey this with any hope of lasting success solely through interpreters, the more so since it was C.M.S. policy to baptise converts only after they could read the Gospel for themselves. Therefore it

---

229   The alien languages of *Swahili* (from the East African Coast), English (officials and Protestant missionaries), and the French of the Catholic White Fathers were irrelevant to the local population at this time in a way that other *Bantu* languages were not.

was vital for the vernacular to be reduced to writing.

It was also natural to suppose that *Runyankore* was spoken by all the people of Ankole, though it was then variously described in the early accounts as *Luima, Luhima,* or *Lunyankole* (the language of *Bahima* tribe or of the Ankole people as a whole). It was difficult for Europeans to learn, and there was uncertainty about whether it was an independent language in itself, or merely just a dialect of *Runyoro-Rutoro.* This was spoken by the people of Toro and Bunyoro which covered large areas of Western Uganda. Indeed there were those who hoped for a *lingua franca* for this part of the country for the sake of achieving unity within Church or State, and some thought *Runyoro-Rutoro* suitable for this purpose. (In a sense they were proved right in the 1990s when *Runyakitara* was to emerge as a "new Language" combining those of *Runyankore-Rukiga* and *Runyoro-Rutoro.*) Others even believed that *Luganda* (spoken by the people of the large territory of Buganda to the east) could eventually become the language for the whole of the south of the Protectorate.

This discussion raised various questions. Would *Runyankore* eventually become redundant? Was it in any way essential apart from the initial contacts? Would Christian texts ever be really needed in it? There was certainly no need of them if the local people could readily understand *Runyoro-Rutoro,* and even perhaps *Luganda.* This discussion is very relevant to the development of Mbarara, and it continued over many years.

As the Churches spread out from Kampala their vernacular remained *Luganda,* for it was the language of the first evangelists who went out to the outlying countries, it alone already possessed the Bible in translation as well as other literature, and it was strongly advocated by some key people. Nevertheless it was largely useless outside of Buganda for anything but casual contact.

Therefore the first real engagement with *Runyankore* was made by the C.M.S. missionaries. However, this was not as clear cut a matter as it first sounds. Morris found that

> the *Bahima* speak the *Bantu* tongue of the *Bairu,* subject only to minor differences in pronunciation and to the fact that the *Bahima* have a certain exclusive vocabulary. ... If

the *Bahima* spoke an Hamitic language when they first entered the area, no trace of this now remains.[230]

However, he also found that a territorial, tonal variation (which was not tribal) could also be recognised. There were other difficulties experienced by J. J. Willis, one of the first C.M.S. missionaries who found it hard to understand people in the country districts. He also mentioned a difference between the *Bahima* chiefs and the "peasant *Bahima*" (which sounds like Morris's tonal variation) after a journey to Isingiro.

> One often wonders if a European will ever really be thoroughly intelligible to them. Like as those two dialects undoubtedly are [*Runyankore* and *Runyoro*] Mrs Fisher, who knows the latter well, could scarcely make out a word of what these porters said: they thicken and slur over all their words, running them into one another [so] that it is exceedingly difficult to recognise a single word. Theirs is practically the same language as that spoken by the *Bahima* chiefs, with a few trifling exceptions; but while the chiefs are bad enough to understand, the peasants are ten times worse. It will take years to get anything approaching their accent.[231]

This was not the experience of a novice, since Willis had been in the country for sixteen months when it was written. At the same time he was aware of really different languages being spoken in some places that he visited:

> In language if in nothing else, Ankole people love variety. On Monday morning in Egara they were talking *Runyankole*. On Monday evening we were in a *Luganda* speaking little colony. The people round in Bunyaruguru, who long ago emigrated from Buganda, finding no language to suit them, speak a language of their own. On Tuesday, down at Kazinga the boatmen were speaking *Lukonjo* – quite a different language [from the Ruwenzori mountain region]. ... And here (Buwehju) where we spent Sunday I think they spoke *Lukonjo*, but cannot be sure, none of us knowing it in the least.[232]

---

[230]   Morris, H. F., *The Heroic Recitations of the Bahima of Ankole*, Oxford (1964), p. 8.

[231]   Willis's Journal, 2/71, 8th April 1902.

[232]   *Ibid*, 2/35 14th November 1901.

Though this certainly represents an over-emphasis of differences, there was a genuine problem. Nevertheless, it was still
realistic to speak of *Runyankore* being the basic vernacular for
the Ankole region.

This being the case, and one, which was soon appreciated
by the missionaries, why was any sustained translation into
Runyankore so long delayed? Four main points stand out in
explanation. Not only did the language have to be reduced to
writing and eventually standardised with *Rukiga* (the language
of the adjoining district of Kigezi), but also its relationship
with neighbouring languages had to be worked out. It was long
felt that *Runyankore* would be eclipsed by one of these, most
probably *Luganda*.

Then there was the political factor. The question of language was also tied up with the relationship between the country of Ankole and other parts of the Protectorate, and this
formed the basis of uncertainty about the association of these
various areas within the Church itself. Here again the influences emanating from Buganda were strong.

Third, the incentive provided by the desire to propagate
the Christian faith was not at first very strongly in favour of
the local vernacular. It was largely hoped by those (from outside Ankole) who made the decisions that literature in another
language (first *Luganda*, and later *Runyoro*) would prove to be
sufficiently satisfactory to make the production of *Runyankore*
versions unnecessary.

Lastly, there was the practical problem of personnel. Even
when the desirability of translating into *Runyankore* was accepted, there was a real problem in finding people able to carry
out the work.

As early as 1897 the C.M.S. missionary, Pilkington, determined to learn *Runyankore* as a necessary step towards ini-
tiating effective evangelisation in Ankole. It is interesting to
speculate on the influence he would have had on the work
there and on translation work in general. However, he was
killed when acting as a translator during the Mutiny soon after
he had been staying with Clayton in Koki, in July 1897. At that
time Archdeacon Walker wrote home on a kindred situation in
Busoga, recommending Pilkington's view that the people
should have the Gospels translated in order to reach them.

Among the missionaries, Pilkington was the one most largely responsible for the translation of the Bible into *Luganda*, which had just been accomplished. His contemporaries held him in considerable awe, and it was typical that they should bow to his opinion in a question of language.

However, with the Christian expansion following the re-establishment of the Protectorate authority after the Mutiny, the language question came to the fore. The rapid expansion in Toro in particular caused this concern. Being the first important example of successful evangelisation within the Protectorate, but outside Buganda, there also arose the suggestion that the Toro situation should be developed into a new C.M.S. Mission. For some, independence in language was seen as a threat to the unity of the developing Church. Archdeacon Walker in particular felt this, and almost the whole of his experience had been in Buganda. His opinion commanded much respect, particularly in London, and in October 1899 he wrote in favour of making "*Luganda* the *lingua franca* throughout the whole of our work here, at any rate in the countries of Uganda, Usoga, Unyoro, Toro, and Ankole."[233]

In this he found himself at variance with younger men who quickly became deeply involved in the areas outside Buganda where they were working. They championed the vernaculars of those regions following the precedent of the books produced for Busoga in the east of the country. Nevertheless Walker had some convincing arguments to support his opinion, besides his strong Buganda orientation. Though modified somewhat in practice by Bishop Tucker, Walker's thinking seems to have remained a powerful factor in missionary policy for many years and certainly can be seen in the way the situation developed in Ankole. In his view the Gospel should be preached in the local language or dialect. He considered that *Luganda* was the best for training the teachers and for printed books. Moreover he believed that local vernaculars were often limited to small numbers of people.[234]

It is easy enough now to view as naive Walker's assump-

---

[233]   *Ibid*, 2/35 14th November 1901.

[234]   *Ibid*.

tion that *Luganda* was the one language best suited to be used
more widely. Nevertheless it must be remembered that at the
time only *Luganda* possessed a body of Christian literature.
Moreover, there were also very strong political and cultural, as
well as religious, reasons why those who were not *Baganda*
should learn the language of that country. After a few months
in Ankole, Willis noted with evident surprise that "*Luganda* is
practically useless: even the chiefs understand very little of it,"
yet "curiously enough everywhere they are most anxious to be
taught in *Luganda*."[235]

For someone like Walker there was nothing odd about expecting a people to be reached in their own vernacular but then
instructed in the Christian faith in another. In Buganda the
teaching had been carried on in *Swahili* for over fifteen years
(up to the end of 1893)[236] although the missionaries had begun
to tackle the learning of *Luganda* from their earliest years in
the country.[237] There was little reason therefore for him to suppose that *Luganda* could not be utilised elsewhere among the
traditional countries, just as *Swahili* had been there.

Moreover, unlike some of his fellows, he remained suita-
bly diffident about the European's ability to learn languages
easily, and to convey his meaning exactly in the vernacular. If
Luganda became a widely used medium, there would be one
set of books with translation steadily improving as that language became more deeply understood. Already there was a
confidence between the Mission and well-taught *Baganda* who
readily "put us right if we make mistakes." In addition, the
small number of missionaries could more easily be moved
around if there was a standard vernacular in which they could
communicate.

After considerable debate among the missionaries, Walker
then reaffirmed his conclusion that initial preaching should be

---

[235]   *Mengo Notes* II/VII, Nov.1901 – CMS G3.A7/02 246. The italics are
his.

[236]   Millar, E. *Uganda Notes*, January 1913, p. 20.

[237]   For instance we find Mackay collecting *Luganda* phrases and idioms,
adding to his vocabulary, and being greatly concerned with accuracy
in 1879 – Harrison, J. W., *Mackay of Uganda* (1890) p. 125.

in the language best known to the people, but saw the use of *Luganda* by missionaries and teachers as a unifying force in the church of the future "to discourage petty jealousies which destroy the sense of unity and undermine our strength."[238] Thus, within three years the missionary leadership had adopted a much more limited attitude towards translations and this greatly affected Ankole.

By the middle of July 1900 the Bishop had formed his opinion and this was later confirmed in the 'Memorandum on Language' drawn up at the C.M.S. London headquarters in Salisbury Square while Tucker was on leave in November 1901. He had far greater experience of areas outside Buganda than Walker and shows a much more accurate understanding of the situation.

Nevertheless, he believed that the C.M.S. had "such an enormous advantage in having the Bible and Prayers in *Luganda* that every effort should be made to widen the field of their circulation." In addition there was the "immense advantage of having a church in which all the various nationalities speak one" tongue. He believed that all the areas he had mentioned "will adopt *Luganda*. Nkole will be a very long while before it does so, but it will come. ..." Despite this comment he "consented to the Gospels being translated and all elementary instruction being given in *Runyoro*" to "meet the present condition of things, the present necessity."

In the long run Tucker's opinion did not turn out to be well founded and the nationalisms he played down came to re-assert themselves. Nevertheless his 'Memorandum'[239] provided the background in which the pioneer work in Ankole was carried on. While the use of *Luganda* was encouraged, the way was open for the use of the local vernacular in a pioneer situation,

---

[238]   Walker to Baylis, 26th Sept.1901 – CMS G3.A7/02 -218.

[238]   *Ibid.*

[239]   All of Tucker's views quoted in these pages come from the Memorandum of the Interview which took place on 8th November 1901 in London between the Bishop and the Secretaries of C.M.S. on the subject of the language problems of the Uganda Mission – CMS G3.A7/02 – 216.

and such matters could be decided locally.

Over the next few years there was considerable experimentation in Ankole, for *Runyankore* was "yet beset with difficulties." Not yet reduced to writing, the translation of the Bible into it would be the work of years, and the printing of a fresh lot of books "immensely expensive."[240]

Thus early European activities in Western Uganda show only a confused appreciation of language. The idea that *Runyankore* was no more than a particular form, or perhaps a dialect, of *Runyoro* persisted from 1901 to the Second World War (with a joint Dictionary published in 1938). Two decades later a more accurate understanding prevailed. Dr Morris, the greatest authority (in print) on the language, summed up the change. Though *Runyankore* is of the *"Runyoro* group" it is "a separate language from *Runyoro* and not merely a dialect of it."[241] (This was not the last word, see *Runyakitara*, page 94).

Wrong assumptions were therefore made in the early years of the twentieth century and these are reflected in the decision that *Runyoro* was sufficiently suitable for full use in Ankole, so that it was unnecessary to treat *Runyankore* as being of totally separate significance. As it was a form of *Runyoro*, it was thought that the cultural and political prejudices against the main language could be overcome. It was also wrong to assume that an illiterate people could cope with something other than their own tongue when learning to read, or even when listening to something read to them. As the situation developed *Runyoro* and *Luganda* were used for teaching purposes, *Luganda* for more advanced teaching, and a smattering of English for the sake of interest or prestige.

A question arises from this. How the did *Runyankore* survive as the language of Ankole without being replaced by *Runyoro*? Part of the answer is that it was by no means entirely rejected by the missionaries, and could not be, for they used it in conversation and in teaching. The personnel of the C.M.S. and the White Fathers both found that they needed *Runyankore* for proper contact with the people. In particular, one of the first

---

[240]   Willis discuss all this in *W.J.* 1.220 – 222, 18th July 1901.

[241]   Morris, H. F. 'Some Aspects of *Runyankore*'. *U.J.* **22/1**, (1958), p. 54.

and the White Fathers both found that they needed *Runyankore*
for proper contact with the people. In particular, one of the first
two female missionaries to Ankole, Theo Baker of the C.M.S.,
found that "the women did not readily learn either *Luganda* or
Runyoro." Therefore she set to work to learn *Runyankore*, and
by 1906 had "collected a vocabulary of about a 1000 words
and also some 200 proverbs."[242]

The Roman Catholics, too, had first used *Luganda*, which
they found ineffective.[243] Both missions, however, only used
the vernacular to lead people on to something else. The found-
er of the Fathers, Cardinal Lavigiere, had laid down that they
should compile a vocabulary and a grammar and "as soon as
possible translate the Gospels and a short catechism."[244] Accordingly Père Gorju, the Superior at Nyamitanga (Mbarara)
from 1902, produced his *Du Ruganda au Runyoro au Runyankole – essai de Grammaire Comparée* in 1906, and later his
Essai de Grammaire Runyankole.[245]

The general Roman Catholic practice[246] was to provide "a
catechism, a simple prayer book, a simple Bible and Church
History." Some of these may have been made available locally
in *Runyankore*. The "simple Bible and Church History" were
certainly available in 1927.[247] Morris writes of Europeans try-

---

242   *Uganda Notes*, VIII/I, January 1907, personalia, p.7; see Appendix A:
Miss Attlee remained only briefly in Ankole, but Mrs Clayton
(married in 1904) had been a C.M.S. missionary herself and remained
with her husband in Mbarara.

243   W.J. 2/129, 31st Oct. 1902.

244   Bouniol, J. *The White Fathers and their Mission,* London, (1929), p.
84.

245   Listed in the Bibliography to Sir John Gray's typescript "A History of
Ankole'" 1952. The British Library has a copy of the first. Gorju's
works were not substantial, and there is no evidence that they provided
in any sense a proper grammar, or were used outside the White
Fathers' circle.

246   Grimshaw, E. A 'Short History of the Vicariate of the Upper Nile' MS
quoted by Gale, H. P. *Uganda and the Mill Hill Fathers*, London
(1959), pp. 236–240.

247   *Amakuru Mahango G'Edini omu Runyankole,* published by the White
Fathers, Entebbe. There is a copy in The Bible House Library.

ing to learn *Runyankore* by using Maddox's *Runyoro* Grammar, or the "grammar of *Ruhaya*, a similar language of Bukoba District, Tanganyika" so that this might have had usefulness in Ankole.[248]

Like the Protestants, the Catholics moved on from a beginning with *Luganda* to *Runyoro*, and for a time preferred this to *Runyankore*. In 1903 prayers were said in *Runyoro* with some concessions to *Runyankore*. However, it was recognised that "this is not one language" because areas like Ibanda, Bunyaruguru, and Igara "have their own patois, which is closer to *Runyoro*." There was a desire for a *lingua franca* for the western areas of the Protectorate,[249] but in 1908 *Runyankore* was "to be used instead of *Luganda*", perhaps referring to the Catechism.[250] The Fathers also found *Runyankore* more difficult than *Luganda*.[251]

There is a curious statement in their Diary for January 1907 that "Clayton never learnt the language."[252] He would have been the last to claim to be a linguistic expert, but the comment does less than justice to one who had recently been largely responsible for completing a translation of St Matthew's Gospel.

HARRY ST GEORGE GALT
His grave at Mbarara Old Church on Kamukuzi hill records that he was "speared by a native Ankole" near Ibanda on 19th May 1905.

---

248   Morris, H. F. & Kirwan, B. E. R. *A Runyankore Grammar*, Kampala (1957), p. xii.

249   'Diary of the Mbarara Mission' by Father (later Bishop) Gorju. (hereafter, Dairy) 5th April 1903. Typescript transcribed from the original, and in The White Fathers' Archive, Rome. Quoted by kind favour of Dr Louise Pirouet.

250   *Ibid*, 11th March 1908, and comment by Dr Pirouet.

251   *Rapport Annuel*, 1905/06 (Year Book of The White Fathers' Mission), information and translation by Dr. Pirouet.

252   Diary, *op. cit.*, 17th January 1907 (Dr Pirouet).

In addition because of the "unsafe" state of the country following the murder of Galt in 1905, it was virtually impossible to itinerate. During this time of enforced reflection the Claytons (he had married in 1904) reconsidered the use of *Runyankore.* First a reading sheet was produced in that language in 1906. The translation of the Gospel of St Matthew was accepted for publication in the following year. Despite inaccuracies, it was recognisably in *Runyankore* and was used as such for many years.[253]

It is interesting that Clayton felt it necessary to produce these in spite of the fact that the New Testament had become available in *Runyoro* in 1905. These early translations into the language are now regarded as rather poor, which, considering the circumstances, and that they are the very first sustained attempt to render it from English, is perhaps not surprising.

The St Matthew was sufficiently helpful[254] to lead W. E. Owen, who came to stand in for Clayton during his second home leave (1907), to attempt St John. On returning to Uganda, Clayton was first sent to Mbale but after having Blackwater Fever it was decided to send him back to Mbarara. With Theo Baker, he was able to revise Owen's work before it was printed in 1910.[255] Clayton left Uganda in 1912, and Owen moved on to Kavirondo where he carried out his life work.

Miss Baker,[256] who had arrived in 1904 and served for nearly twenty years, continued with her interest in translation. In 1913 she is described as "our best *Runyankore* scholar at

---

253 *Matayo omu Lunyankole,* British & Foreign Bible Society, London (1907) *St Matthew's Gospel* translated by H. Clayton of CMS, pp. 82. Slightly revised by M. T. Baker, (1918). It was only replaced in 1962 by *Endegaano Ensya* (The New Testament) translated by A. C. Stanley Smith, Lazaro Tabaro, P. Kareebya, and E. Mugimba.

254 'The *Runyankore-Rukiga* Bible Notes on File' BFBS, London. Note 2 quotes a letter from the Revd E. Millar, Kampala, to Dr Kilgour, Editorial Superintendent, 25th August 1910: "The Gospel of St Matthew ... has been much appreciated in the country." Millar was a very experienced missionary, who would know. *Ibid,* 17th January 1907 (Dr Pirouet).

255 *Ibid.*

256 See below note 263.

present"[257] and her translations of *St Mark* and *St Luke* appeared in 1915. This led to a request for the whole of the New Testament to be rendered into *Runyankore*. The Church Council of the Ankole Rural Deanery applied on 27th July 1915 for this to be carried out, though Willis (who by then had succeeded Tucker as Bishop) vetoed the plan when it came to the Diocesan Council.[258] That delayed the task for forty years.

Whatever the shortcomings of these early translations, they were the beginnings of a literature in *Runyankore*, and they were used. Any further translation into the language by the Protestant missionaries was inhibited by the difficulty in finding a translator. The work in this field by the White Fathers, though important, was seemingly less substantial.

Little further was achieved until after the Second World War when the expansion of a literature in *Runyankore* came not from translation, or specifically Christian motivation. New works were then published by the East African Literature Bureau, the first of them becoming available in 1948. These were mostly by indigenous authors writing directly in their own language.[259] A *Runyoro-Runyankore* Dictionary had been published in 1938.[260] Then reflecting the clear acknowledgement that Ankole had a separate language, a *Runyankore-Rukiga* Dictionary came out in 1959 soon after the *Runyankore* Grammar.[261]

---

[257]   *Ibid.* Note 4 quoting Millar, E. to B.F.B.S, 28th August 1913.

[258]   Minutes of the Diocesan Council (Uganda) 1914 (4 Nov.) to 1918; among the Registers at St James's Cathedral, Mbarara, p. 50 under Quarterly Meeting 12th January 1916 Item 1 (postponed from the meeting 6th October 1915 because the Rural Dean was not present) and p. 67 under Quarterly Meeting, 5th April 1916 Item 2.

[259]   *Abakozire Eby'Okutangaaza Omuri Ankole* (Some Eminent People of Ankole) by K. K. Nganwa (1948, 1949, 1966) was the first of these, and in 1970 I made a list of fourteen such titles. Longmans, Nelson and other untraced sources, published another eight titles (*forthcoming*).

[260]   *A Lunyoro-Lunyankole-English and English-Lunyoro-Lunyankole Dictionary*, by Miss M. B. Davis, London S.P.C.K.

[261]   *A Simplified Runyankore-Rukiga-English and English-Runyankore-Rukiga Dictionary*, by C. Taylor, E.A.L.B.

The final vindication of *Runyankore* as a language distinct from *Runyoro*, came with the publication of the translation of the whole of the Bible in 1964, over half a century after it had been available in that rival tongue.[262] Herbert Clayton may not have been a noted linguist but he was a deeply committed missionary, and the success of his pioneering translation of St Matthew's Gospel ensured that the identity of *Runyankore* would be preserved and a literature developed.

Learning the language was always a team effort between different peoples. Similarly the eventual translation of the Bible was the result of collaboration between Africans and a European, as was the very first book to appear in the language of Ankole in its modern centre at Mbarara.

Note on Miss Baker[263]

Mabel Theodora Baker was a strong character, who served for four tours in Ankole from June 1903 until July 1920. Locally she was known as *Amoti*. She independently funded herself in Uganda. A cousin of the author Ryder Haggard,[264] she came from a family of Royal Engineer officers. Her father and brother were General W. A., and Colonel W. W. Baker. A nephew survived serving in the First World War in which he took to the air. He went on to become an Air Vice Marshal, and was Chief of Staff, Mediterranean Allied Air Force 1944–45, retiring in 1946. Miss Baker lived to see all this, for, retiring from the C.M.S. in 1924, she lived on at home until 1948. The Claytons had first met her at the C.M.S. headquarters in London, and remembered her as "the dog and bicycle lady." They were rather alarmed on hearing that she was coming to Mbarara. However, they soon appreciated her sterling qualities, and after only six weeks wrote home to say that they were very lucky to have her.

---

[262] *Baibuli Erikwera,* the Bible translated by A. C. Stanley Smith, CMS, L. Tabaro, P. Kareebya, E. Mugimba, and a representative committee, BFBS London, (1964); cf. *Ekitabu Ekirukwera ekya Ruhanga ekibeta Baibul,* the Bible translated by H. E. Maddox, BFBS, London (1912).

[263] Compiled from C.M.S. sources and contact with the family.

[264] C. L. 24th December 1904.

CHAPTER TEN

WHEN DID MBARARA BECOME A TOWN?

The question of when Mbarara first became a town needs some discussion. This is probably more complex than might be expected. One geographer of East Africa has summed up the situation very realistically: 'there is no general agreement on what constitutes a town.'[265] This being so, there will always be those who will look for an interpretation of the term which will provide grounds for finding a long history of urban life in the East African interior. For such, even the *orurembo* of Ntare, traditional, temporary, and dependent on herding and raiding though it was, will be a town. In the article mentioned at the beginning,[266] Dr Twaddle cited two authorities. Professor Oliver and Dr Gutkind, in support of this view, though as the latter refers to the exceptional areas of West Africa and the East Africa coast the connection is not obvious in this case.[267]

To be fair to the members of the Royal Commission and their Report, it should be noted, that, though their comment on the growth of towns forms only one paragraph, they were careful to find exceptions in both the coastal ports and the headquarters of the hereditary chiefs north and west of lake Victoria. Moreover they added two reservations to this second exception (i) that these were "temporary growths" and (ii) that they "bore no resemblance to the permanent urban centre as we know it today."[268] Obviously these were generalisations, and to the first of them some exceptions may be found, but

---

265   O'Connor, A. M. 'The distribution of towns in sub-Saharan Africa' in J. Gugler, 'Urban growth in sub-Saharan Africa', (*Nkanga* no. 6), p. 5.

266   See note 11.

267   Gutkind, P. C. W., 'Town life in Buganda', (*UJ, 20,* 1956, p. 37).

268   Royal Commission, *op. cit.,* p. 200.

these do not prove that settlement comparable to the modern urban centre has a long history in the East African interior. It is the more generally accepted view that urban development in sub-Saharan Africa is recent.[269]

This view takes into account the more conventional factors which are looked for in defining townships. In addition to the settlement of a considerable number of people on one site, some of these include evidence of more than an agricultural way of life, and the presence of some trade, possibly of industry as well. Other points such as nodality, and reasonable permanence, are also likely to be expected. Set in this wider context it can hardly be maintained that Ntare's *orurembo* constituted a town. Nor is it the contention of this article that Macallister's Mbarara was a town either. What is claimed is that these wider factors were beginning to be recognizable before he left, and that on this foundation grew up the community which developed into a town.[270]

Two further points need to be made in the light of Dr Twaddle's conclusions about Mbale. Firstly that, apart from ivory and powder, trade did follow the 'Flag' in Ankole, it did not come first. Dr Cook's mother expressed this rather quaintly when describing his first visit (December 1899) from his let-

---

[269]   Gugler, *op. cit.,* p. 3.

[270]   There is currently a good deal of discussion, especially amongst geographers, on the definition of urban origins and the process and dispersal of urbanisation. Gideon Sjoberg, *The pre-industrial city,* gives a certain emphasis to the economic role and especially to the emergence of a specialist class of craftsmen and tradesmen with non-agricultural roles. It could be feasible to argue that political and administrative functions implied a similar presence of a specialist, non-agricultural class. More recently Paul Wheatley, *The pivot of the four quarters; a preliminary enquiry into* and *character of the ancient Chinese city,* has argued from Chinese evidence that the main motivation for urban origin is by the peasantry for a cosmo-magical symbol, and that cities have emerged as ceremonial centres as a microcosm of cosmic reality. Thus he advances religion rather than economics as the prime variable. Clearly the place of cities in Africa are relevant to certain aspects of this discussion and Akin Mabogunje has commented upon the character of Yoruba towns, *Urbanisation in Nigeria and Yoruba towns.* (Note contributed by Professor B. W. Langlands in 1973.)

ters. "At last they reached Fort Imbarara, where the Union Jack was floating in the wind, and after a kind and hospitable reception from the resident in charge [Macallister], they pressed on to the native king's capital. ..."[271] This would seem a completely jingoistic description were it not for the fact that there was really nothing else at the station to describe and certainly nothing in the way of a trading centre.

Secondly, there is the question of the purpose of such enquiries as this. It is easy to understand, and right to commend, the re-establishing of the validity of things African, including the nature of African settlement and community. Yet there is a great danger that the *alien* nature of much urban growth in East Africa may be played down for the wrong reasons. Most eastern African towns are the result of the encounter between the different cultures African, Asian and European. To pretend otherwise is to do a disservice to the present inhabitants. Dr O'Connor has wisely stated that

> it is therefore suggested that the pattern of town growth should be examined and understood in each country, in order that governments may have a sound basis upon which to frame their policies in this field.[272]

The lot of those who live in modern urban Ankole will not be improved by pressing the connection between the cattle-*kraal* of a pastoral king with the permanent urban centre as it is known today and will develop tomorrow.

In conclusion therefore it can be said that continuous occupation of the site on which Mbarara stands began when Macallister arrived to set up the headquarters for Ankole District. Almost at once it acquired a multifarious importance as an administrative centre for central and local government; as the base for both army and police in the area; as the location of embryo scientific medical facilities; as a route centre; as a place of trade and the collection of tax; as the headquarters of both Protestant and Roman Catholic Churches; as a market for local produce, and as a place where a rudimentary educational

---

[271]   Cook, H. B., A *doctor and his dog in Uganda*, (London, R.T.S., (1903), p. 128 from a letter of 9 December 1899.

[272]   O'Connor, *op. cit.*, p. 11.

system was beginning. A visitor in 1903 described it as

A pretty place, well kept and neatly laid out, with good roads [this is before the days of motor transport], lined on either side by trees. The bungalows are comfortable and well built. They are each enclosed in large compounds. With the exception of Entebbe, Mbarara is by far the pleasantest and the most civilized station in the whole of the Uganda Protectorate. The military lines, the magazine and the fort, are on the highest point of the hill. A little lower down, are the Civil Offices and quarters and, on another hill opposite, are the Police lines, the hospital, jail, etc.

By this time (1903) "the English officials consist of a Sub-Collector and a Doctor, with two Officers in command of ... the detachment stationed at Mbarara ... formed by two Companies of the Uganda Rifles."[273]

'*BAGANDA* SOLDIERS of the King's African Rifles'

Within just a few years Mbarara was of sufficient importance to be named by the Government as a Township on the 26th June 1906, along with ten other towns in Uganda headed by Kampala.[274] The least that can be said is that by this time it had become sufficiently established, and such municipal status has continued to expand ever since. Mbarara was then defined as "the area ex-

---

[273] Garstin, *op. cit.* p.34. footnote 1 adds there that "in these Companies are 180 Soudanese, and 70 Waganda" and "100 Police." The Uganda Rifles were just being reformed as part of the King's African Rifles.

[274] Ennis, G. F. M. and Carter, W. Morris, *Laws of the Uganda Protectorate in force on 31 December 1909.* Entebbe, G.P., (1910), n. 310.

tending northwards from the river Ruizi comprised within a circle having a radius of one mile with the Collector's present office as centre."

In his Medical Report for that same year (1906) Dr Lowsley divided it into four areas "European quarters, troops, missions, and natives."[275] Strictly speaking, according to the Township Proclamation, only the first two of these came within the area laid down. However Dr Lowsley's analysis seems to be more realistic, though he included traders under his first heading because of their proximity to those quarters.

In 2014 Mbarara is often described as a city rather than a town. This more prestigious term can be used rather vaguely to describe a very large municipality. More precisely it is a large town, with its city status conferred by the state authority. In some parts of the world it has also been usual for it to contain a cathedral. It is still officially stated that there is only one city in Uganda, together with twenty-two large municipalities described as "secondary cities."[276] In 2013 the Physical Structure Committee of the Uganda Parliament was requesting the Government to speed up the creation of new cities in places like Mbarara, Mbale, Gulu, Masaka, and Jinja.[277] Therefore, such formal official recognition seems likely to be given soon.

In concluding this account of the founding of Mbarara perhaps any readers will forgive a personal reminiscence of my Ntare days. It is now first written down more than "forty years on" but remains a vivid memory, as does so much else from those familiar parts. Though the School Governors were seeking a Church of Uganda Chaplain, I had to be recruited as someone who could teach 'A' level English, amongst other things and "who happened to be in Anglican Orders." Whenever I had a class of new arrivals, fresh from their Primary Schools scattered throughout the land, I always began by setting an easy essay subject in which they could all say something of themselves. One such response contained a sentence

---

[275] Lowsley, L. D., *op. cit.* p. 4.

[276] There are many articles on web-sites about the need for a clear urbanisation policy in which Mbarara always seems to be included.

[277] Report on the Agora-parl.org web-site 28 August 2013.

worth repeating now.

The boy described the overwhelming sense of awe which smote him when he first entered Mbarara, previously having known only a rural life in which villages were the largest settlement. He set down on paper this vivid exclamation:

"When I first saw Mbarara, I fell as one dead!"

That must be my reaction, too, were I ever to return to this 'city', having only ever known it as a small town. My pioneering predecessors, like Macallister and Clayton, would feel it far more acutely in their astonishment, but the horror of Ntare V and Igumira would be beyond description. Little more than a dozen decades ago it was only briefly the site of the *Omugabe*'s itinerating *orurembo* set within the grasslands once rich in *mburara*.

Conclusion

The role of Asian traders in their *dukas* was still legendary in 1970. They could establish themselves in remote areas, survive "on a shoe-string", and often prosper. They seemed to have contacts all over the world through which they could import almost anything. They were also excellent artisans.[278] Some of these skills have been apparent in the founding of Mbarara.

The *Banyankore* were, of course, overwhelmingly paramount in numbers. Their titular head, the *Omugabe*, was *Rubambansi* Edwardi Sulemani Kahaya II. His part is often overshadowed by the progressive behaviour of *Owekitiinisa* Nuwa Mbaguta, the *Enganzi*. Nevertheless, while still a very young man emerging from the controlling hands of his

---

[278] The writer will always have vividly memories of Christmas 1971. The *coup* in January had already begun to cause unusual difficulties. We enjoyed piped water from the tank on the hilltop site of the old fort on one of the Muti hills above the golf course. Machinery there had broken down, and we were now being supplied by water carts. The spare parts needed could only been found in Nairobi. The Asian engineer (among those expelled in the following summer) made the journey at all possible speed. I shall always remember waking up on Christmas morning to the joyful sound of water once again flowing into the tank in our roof.

Regents, Kahaya made the decision to move his *orurembo* from Rushasha to Kamukuzi in 1899.[279] This was truly remarkable, being in opposition to the policy of his two elders, one of them his own father. Both would have preferred to have rejected any concept of "Uganda". Without his action, Ankole District would have had two capitals, wherever his *kraal* was located, and the Administration at Mbarara. His change of heart signalled co-operation, and the fledgling town was free to develop into what it has now become.

Foremost among the few Europeans was Macallister. He may not have been much of a success as a husband and father because of his absorption in Uganda, but there is still to his credit a major role in the founding of the modern municipality of Mbarara.

The part played by others among the indigenous people has already been adequately demonstrated, including some *Baganda* and the Sudanese from further afield. Since those early days, countless others have been involved in what has since been achieved.

---

[279] See above, note 144.

APPENDIX A

EUROPEAN TRAVELLERS IN ANKOLE 1876–1901

This chapter is concerned with the first contacts between Europeans and the people of Ankole. The quarter of a century between 1876–1901 is significant. It began with Stanley as the first known to have set foot in the country, and ended with the signing of the Ankole Agreement. Of course the African personalities involved are equally important, but had not travelled thousands of miles into a strange environment, and anyway they would best be researched within Uganda. The Europeans were the incomers, few in number, and coming for specific reasons. Their background is best inquired into within their own continent, as we shall see. Included here are the names of all those known to have visited any part of the country during this period, for whatever purpose. The earliest of them were basically explorers. Some of those who followed on in the service of the Imperial British East Africa Company, and then of the Uganda Protectorate Administration were also in some sense explorers too. Whether they were administrative, military, or commercial personnel, they ventured into parts of the country not previously known to have been crossed by any one of their race. Apart from them there are also the Christian missionaries.

Summary Listing All Europeans Known to Have Entered Any Part of Ankole During This Period

Information is set out in this way on the following pages:

First of all, the individual names are listed in chronological order; then the sources are quoted to show their presence in Ankole. The information given in this Appendix also appears in the writer's *Ankole Religion and Christianity*. There it is greatly expanded accompanied by some outline of the circumstances of their time spent in Ankole, before biographical details are provided wherever possible for the individuals involed. There the names follow the same order as in the Summary here.

There is no attempt to provide an exhaustive list of references, only to establish that the journey was made. Wherever possible the earliest authority has been cited.

In the following Table, a single * indicates a fatality during that tour, and a double ** death in Africa later or as a result of serving there.

Ref.	Date	Travellers	Representing	Route	Nature of Contact
a	Jan 76	H.M.Stanley F.Pocock*	*New York Herald Daily Telegraph*	Northern Nkore	No contact with *Omugabe*
b	July 89	H.M.Stanley, again W.Hoffman Emin Pasha** T.H.Parke** A.J.Mounteney-Jephson R.H.Nelson** W.G.Stairs** W.Bonny G.Casati	Emin Pasha Relief Expedition	Fort George -Bukoba passing near the *orurembo* at Muti	*Omukago* with Bucunku (for Ntare V) and Stanley's claim of a 'treaty'
c	Apr 91	Emin Pasha, again	Imperial German Administration	Bukoba-Rwampara-Kigezi-west side of Lake Edward	Emin wrote to Ntare, who sought alliance with Germans, but Langheld (at Bukoba) refused
d	Apr 91	F.Stuhlmann, following Emin	The same	As for Emin	None
e	June-July 91	F.J.D.Lugard Dr J.S. Macpherson W.Grant	Imperial British East Africa Company	Northern Nkore	Treaty & *omukago* with Birere (for Ntare)
f	Oct 91	W.F. De Winton*	Lugard's party	The same	

g	Dec 91	Lugard, again returning		Lake Edward-Buganda	
h	Jan-Feb 92	Stuhlmann, again		Returning to Bukoba	
i	1892-93	C.S.Reddie	I.B.E.A.C.	Northern Nkore	None: surveying party
J	Sept 93	W.Langheld	Imperial German Adm at Bukoba	Fort George-Bukoba	*Omukago* with Ntare by messenger at Bukoba
k	Mar-Apr 94	G.F.Scott Elliot	Personal Botanical Expedition	Karagwe - Toro	He sent presents, refused *omkago*; Ntare provided guide
l	July 94	G.G. Cunningham	Uganda Protectorate	Fort George to Koki via 'Ntali's'	Treaty - *omukago* declined
m	Feb 95	See below			
n	Aug 96	See below			
o	1897	See below			
p	1897 & 1898	C.G.H.Sitwell** C.V.C.Hobart W.H. Abdul Malek*	Various U.P. patrols hunting rebels	Mainly in North & East Nkore	Ultimatums – no Treaty or *omukago*
q	Early in 98	R.T. Kirkpatrick*	Uganda Rifles	Northern Nkore	Surveying – no contact reported
r	May 98	See below			
s	Aug-Oct 98	M.J.Tighe	U.P. Administration	Eastern Nkore	No meeting recorded
t	Nov 98	R.J.D. Macallister**	U.P.Adm	Buddu - Karwera – *orurembo* (Rushasha)	First European encounter with *Omugabe* (Kahaya)

u	Dec 98	Macallister again R.Baile * A.A.Fisher ** H.C. Moorhouse	U.P.Adm Uganda Rifles „		Return, with military escort to set up the initial British Administration in Ankole.
v	May 99	H.Clayton	Church Missionary Society	Koki-Mbarara-*orurembo* at Rushasha	First mission-ary reconnais-sance to meet the *Omugabe*
w	Dec 99	A.R.Tucker A.R.Cook	C.M.S. „	Koki-Mbarara-Toro	First Bishop & doctor to meet *Omugabe*
x	June 99	R.R.Racey	U.P. Adm	Throughout Ankole	Official Duties
y	Feb-Mar 00	S.W.Ormsby**	Boustead Ridley	Buddu-Mbarara-Toro	First visit by first European Traders
z	Oct 00	G.C.R.Mundy	U.Rifles	Throughout Ankole	Official Duties
aa	Apr 00	Victor M.Manara	U.P.Adm	Throughout Ankole	Official Duties
bb	Aug 00	Sir H.H. Johnston	U.P.Adm	Toro-Mbarara-Toro	The Special Commission-er- official visit
cc	Sept 00	H.Clayton again	C.M.S.	Koki-Mbarara	Temporary visit
dd	Oct 00	J.E.Lesbros Bro.Hermann	White Fathers „	Buddu-Mbarara-Shema	Reconnaiss-ance for their Mission
ee	Jan 01	H.Clayton again J.J.Willis	C.M.S.	Throughout Ankole	Starting mission
ff	Feb 01	G. Wood	Instructor of Police (Sgt. U.R.)	Throughout Ankole	In charge of newly formed police
gg	Jun 01	H.E.Maddox Mrs Maddox	C.M.S. Toro	Toro-Mbarara	Temporary visit

hh	July-Sept 01	Geo.Wilson Mrs Wilson	U.P.Adm	Toro-Mbarara-Toro	Official visit & signing the Ankole Agreement
ii	Sept 01	H.StG.Galt*	U.P.Adm	Throughout Ankole	Official duties

Abdul Malek and Manara might not be strictly Europeans, but were there entirely because of European involvement and in that service. The number of deaths is very high. Of the forty-five individual names listed here, nearly one third (fourteen) died as a result of working in Africa. Three died through violence including the only death within Ankole, though Baile died having just completed a tour there and before he could reach the coast. Of the rest, blackwater fever and dysentery were the main causes of death. The following comparison is not exact because it is over a period and not a single day, but the proportion of fatal loss is far greater than in the "bloodiest day of the British army" at the Battle of the Somme on the 1st July 1916.

There are four sections in the Table marked with the reference "See below'. These are explained here:

m   February 1895: U.P. Expedition planned, but failed to materialise because of lack of manpower.

n   August 1896: U.P. Expedition planned, but failed to materialise because of lack of manpower.

o   1897: U.P. Expedition planned, but failed to materialise because of the *Kabaka* Mwanga's rebellion which was followed by the Sudanese Mutiny.

r   May 1898: U.P. Expedition planned to send Macallister to Ankole, but very unlikely that he went at this time.

References

No attempt has been made to make these exhaustive. The aim has been to establish that the journey was made, and wherever possible citing the earliest reference

a. Stanley, H.M. *Through the Dark Continent,* London (1878), vol. 1 pp. 432ff.

b. Stanley, H.M. *op. cit.,* London (1890), vol. 2 chapter 32. Treaty printed in Gray, J.M. *UJ* 12/1 (1948), pp. 31–32.

c. Schweitzer, G. *The Life and Work of Emin Pasha,* London (1898), vol. 2. pp. 170–198 (quoting vol. 5 of Emin's *Tagebucher*). He passed north of Lat.1°·south, through Kirere, Ruhanga, and Karo. *Ibid* for Ntare's request for help received by Emin (Emin's letter 20 Jan. '91); and Gray, Sir J. M. 'Anglo-German Relations in Uganda 1890-1892', *Journal of African History* 1/2 (1960) p. 294, for Langheld's reaction.

d. Schweitzer *ibid.*

e. Lugard, F.J.D. *op. cit.* (1893), vol. 2 pp. 136 and 160. Perham, M. and Bull, M. *op. cit.,* London (1959), II pp. 210–227. Treaty: printed in Morris, H.F. *op. cit.* (1962) pp. 47–48.

f. Perham & Bull, *ibid* pp. 400 & 407.

g. *Ibid,* pp. 441–450.

h. It is not entirely clear that Stuhlmann went through any part of modern Ankole. He passed further south than on the outward journey with Emin and on this part of the journey ventured north only as far as Lat.1°·south at "Kisuro" in modern Kigezi. From there he made his way directly to Bukoba. Thus he probably passed through part of the modern *saza* of Kajara, but in any case in 1892 this was no part of Nkore, being included in the independent country of Mpororo, vide Stuhlmann, F. *Mit Emin Pascha ins Herz von Afrika*, Berlin (1894), Band 2, kap.27 and *Übersichtskarte der Expedition des Dr. Emin Pascha 1890-92* Gezeichnet von Dr. Richard Kiepert, included among the maps at the end of that volume.

i. Thomas, H.B. and Spencer, A.E. *op. cit.* (1938) p. 4; Macdonald's Map.

j. Langheld, *op. cit.,* (1909) (quoted in Gray *op. cit.* 1952 pp. 58–61.

k. Scott Elliot, G.F. *op. cit.* (1896) chapter 5.

l. Cunningham, G.G. to Commissioner, Port Alice (Entebbe) 24 September 1894 with accompanying 'Description of country passed through…' ESA A.2/3 cf. Colville, H.E., *op. cit.* (1895) pp. 287ff. Treaty in Morris, (1962) *op. cit.*

m. Jackson, F.J. (acting Commissioner) to Secretary of State (Kimberley) Entebbe 8 February 1895, F.O.2/92.

n. "The Government are going to send an armed expedition to Ankole to stop the slave raiding." Leakey, R.H. circular letter from Koki, 26 August 1896, CMS G3.A5/013-4.

o. Berkeley (Commissioner) to F.O. Kampala, 19 November 1896, ESA A.34/2/123 he writes of the 'King of Koki' becoming incorporated into Uganda as a territorial chief, and adds: "It is somewhat difficult to say whether the territories of Toru and Ankole will follow the example led by Koki, I am inclined to think that Toru probably will do so before very long. As regards Ankole, however, where the position of affairs is somewhat unsettled since the death of Ntali ... and the population are less in touch with Uganda than is the case with Koki and Toru, it is probable that some little time must elapse before the situation is sufficiently settled for such a question to usefully come under consideration.

I hope that before long it will be possible to provide an officer and the necessary garrison for the establishment of a station in Ankole. This measure is greatly needed, both for the repression of contraband trade in powder and caps, and the slave raiding which, it cannot well be doubted, still continues over the German frontier."

p. *vide* Weekes, (1973) *op. cit.* pp. 31–2, quoted above in note 11.

q. "Macdonald' map of Uganda 1900 indicates that Kirkpatrick made a substantial new passage across Ankole, south of the Katonga river: this journey must have been undertaken in the early part of 1898." Langlands, B.W. 'Early Travellers in Uganda' *UJ* **26/1** (1962), p. 65.

r. Macallister to Tomkins (private letter) Port Victoria, 6th May 1898 "I leave to go to Ankole." ESA A.4/11/302-3 (between).

s. Tighe, M.J. to Adjutant, 27 Baluchi Light Infantry. 4th January 1899, ESAA.4/15/2.

t. *vide* discussion in Thesis *op. cit.* pp. 216–223.

u. Macallister to Berkeley, 1st January 1899 ESA A.3/15/20; 'Macallister and Mbarara' *op. cit.* p. 38.

v. C. L., 24th, 25th, and 29th May 1899.

w. Tucker, *op. cit.* Vol. 2 pp. 232 and 236–237.

x. Mundy replaced Moorhouse as the Uganda Rifles subaltern under Fisher. He arrived at the Coast, 9th May 1899 (ESA A.4/18/449, Mombasa 26th June 1899). Presumably he had a period of familiarisation at HQ before being sent to Ankole. He is first mentioned by Macallister on 26th October 1899 writing of a "sub chief on the Ankole border who came in here with Mr Mundy" – the chief being under arrest as a rebel (ESA A.4/22/924); it may therefore be that Mr Mundy only arrived in Mbarara in that month. Moorhouse was still active in Ankole under Fisher in May 1899, Macallister to Ternan, 2nd June 1899 ESA A.4/17/264a, but by the following February he was in Iganga, acting as Collector for Busoga, Moorhouse to Johnston, 16th February 1900, ESA A.4/25/104.

y. Johnston, H. H. to Macallister, 9th January 1900, ESA A.5/9/23: Macallister to Johnston, 12th February 1900, ESA A.4/25/122. The first says both men were going to Ankole, the second only mentions Ormsby in Mbarara. It is therefore not clear that Chambers actually reached Mbarara.

z. Report for 'Ankole District Report for June 1900', ESA A/4/29//with 640.

aa. Racey to Commissioner No.C/57, Mbarara, 1st December 1900, ESA A.15/1/40, he brings to "favourable notice Mr. Victor M. Manara, clerk" who has carried out his duties "more responsibly than those usually entrusted to a clerk" and has "on two occasions taken entire charge of Mbarara." The sum of Rs 900 was paid to the Clerk in Ankole in the half year ended 30th September 1900, though this item had not been in the Estimates. Manara therefore can be presumed to have arrived at Mbarara after the beginning of April 1900.

bb. References to Johnston visiting Mbarara are very sparse. There is internal evidence from his book, *op. cit.* Racey to Commissioner No.C/28, Mbarara 23rd August 1900, ESA A.15/1/14 writes of forty-five men enlisted for the new police Force in Ankole and adds, "The English sergeant, to whom you referred when here, would now be of the greatest service in training these men. ..." Clayton in Koki had been expecting Johnston to come in that direction having concluded his visit to Ankole, but "The Commissioner Sir Harry Johnston is not going to pass through Koki and Budu after all. He went from Toro to Ankole and spent four days there and then returned to Toro, whence he hopes to return to Mengo by way of Bunyoro. The officers at Masaka think that the snow mountain Ruwenzori in Toro has an attraction for him." C.L 3rd September 1900.

cc. C.L. 21th September 1900.

dd. 'Ankole District Report for October 1900', ESA

A.15/1/30, "On 28th two missionaries, White Fathers, arrived and have since gone to look about the district." For more detailed references, see Weekes, *Ankole Religion and Christianity*.

ee. Racey to Commissioner, Mbarara 5th January 1901, ESA A/14/1/2: "two representatives of the Church Missionary Society, Messrs H. Clayton and Willis arrived here today."

ff. Ankole District Report for February 1901, ESA A.15/1/28, Wood arrived on 22nd "To instruct the Ankole Constabulary Force."

gg. Ankole District Report for June 1901. ESA A.15/2.54: many other references in C.L. and W.J. for that month.

hh. The Wilsons arrived at Mbarara on 24th July 1901, W.J.1/224 26th August 1901, and left on 14 September, 'Ankole District Report for September 1901', ESA A.15/2 with 75.

ii. The Ankole Report for September also shows that Galt arrived at Mbarara to take over as Collector on 12th, two days before the Wilsons left.

Annie Kate Attlee (1879–1934) and Mabel Theodora Baker (1864–1948), the first European women to work permanently in Ankole, arrived in 1903. Miss Attlee was educated at Wimbledon High School and in Eastbourne. She received her missionary training at The Olives and worked in Uganda from 1903–33, initially in Ankole, but after less than a year she was posted to Toro. She died in the year after retiring. Miss Baker was a trained nurse aged about thirty-eight (see above note 255). Both served as C.M.S. missionaries, and neither ever married.

APPENDIX B

DATING THE FIRST ENCOUNTER WITH AN
OMUGABE FROM POSTAL FRANKINGS

We can now return to the matter of the unusual clue to the precise date of the first face-to-face encounter between an *Omugabe* and a European.

In March 1976 I was approached by Roy Dunstan, the editor of *The Bulletin of the East Africa Study Circle*, over the location of certain mission sites in Uganda, and the ensuing correspondence revealed that he possessed covers addressed to Macallister at a London address, Heathfield, Plumstead, S.E. Dunstan suspected (and it was easily confirmed from the handwriting) that these had been sent by the administrator in East Africa to himself at the London address of his parents. It was also suggested that this had been done on a considerable scale with a view to the likely philatelic value of such material.

The embryo Uganda Protectorate Administration did not have any postage stamps by which letters could be sent. Two C.M.S. missionaries provided the first official stamps on their own machines. Copies of these are now very collectable, but originally they were not regarded seriously by philatelists. Nevertheless they really were used for that purpose until the first officially produced stamps could be made available. That Macallister had a serious profit motive in mind has always seemed to me rather unlikely because he cannot have hoped that the commercial value of such material would ever be very great in his day. That rather murky suggestion is coloured by the sharp contrast provided by their value seventy years on (which is greater still now after over a century).

It is surely more likely that he appreciated the curiosity interest in having to correspond with valid postage stamps, which were produced so amateurishly, especially when there was considerable doubt at the time whether these 'stamps' would ever be accepted by collectors as genuine postage material. He may have had no other purpose in mind than having them among his souvenirs of Uganda. This is even more likely if he was aware that these amateur, but valid, stamps were about to be replaced by proper printed official ones.[280] The earliest examples were produced by the Reverend E. Millar in 1896 on his typewriter, but soon afterwards some more sophisticated examples were printed by the Reverend F. Rowling on his press "at Luba's". These were still only composed of black type lettering on plain paper. By the end of 1898, officially printed postage stamps bearing the head of Queen Victoria were ready to be introduced.

There is another possible reason for Macallister to address letters to himself at his parents' home. We have seen that the previous year he had been refused permission to marry. Perhaps he felt that he could not therefore write direct to his girl friend at her home. If his family removed his letters from the Uganda 'cover' and inserted them in fresh envelopes and sent them on from London, the Uganda origin would be unknown except to the recipient. If this seems far-fetched, it has to be explained how Macallister somehow maintained the relationship and was successful in winning his chosen bride when next on leave.

Be that as it may, Macallister's use of Rowling stamps

---

[280] The writer gathered his own small collection of such souvenirs while in Uganda, with a particular interest in currency. He queued at Grindlay's Bank in Mbarara during the last week in which Imperial banknotes were still valid and obtained some of different denominations. Similarly he had framed as a wall hanging examples of all the coinage going right back to cowrie shells, and for good measure a Maria Theresa Dollar and Zanzibari pice, since the Uganda Protectorate originally extended well into what is now Kenya. Fortunately this was done with no thought of future financial gain as all his Uganda 'treasures' were lost when his home was destroyed by fire in 2011. Nevertheless he is amazed at how much they would have accrued in value over the forty years had they still existed, see p. 71.

occurred shortly before the first official Government stamps came into use superseding the hand made "missionary" ones. The latter therefore would soon become a passing piece of memorabilia, probably likely to have little more value than a certain curiosity, but nevertheless of interest as a souvenir of one's service. The *Stanley Gibbons Catalogue* for 1899 gives no commercial value to the typewritten stamps, and only spasmodically for some of the Rowling.[281]

For our purposes it is of great interest that there are still in existence some of the Rowling stamps which have been franked with the date stamp "Ankole – No 20 98"[282] It is most curious that postage stamps should exist with a postmark from Ankole four weeks before Macallister arrived at Mbarara to set up the permanent station there on the 18th December. As Her Majesty's Sub-Commissioner for the new District and Vice-Consul he would have been responsible for the mail. Proper date-stamps were only introduced in the Protectorate late in 1898, so that presumably one was made for Ankole on the ground that it was expected that Administration would shortly be established there.[283]

---

[281] pp. 212–213 in the catalogue, where the unusually high value of five rupees is listed at twenty-five shillings, one rupee at five shillings and one anna at only sixpence. These figures are in no way exceptional compared with those for the Turks Islands and Victoria on the same pages.

[282] In March 1976 Mr Roy Dunstan's collection included two 8 anna stamps and a one rupee, all bearing this postmark, none of which appear to have been gummed on to the envelope for postal use. He also had a one rupee stamp bearing the postmark "Ankole JA 5 99" (5th January 1899) which had apparently been used postally. He also knew of the existence of a number of covers, that is envelopes bearing such stamps, addressed by Macallister to himself in London.

[283] They had been ordered from Messrs. Waterlow & Sons, London, in 1897: Phillips, C.J. 'The Postage Stamps of Uganda'. This first appeared as two articles in *the Stanley Gibbons Monthly Journal* for February 1904, pp. 166–72, and March 1904, pp.189–192. They were reprinted in *Africa* (Royal Philatelic Society of London) vol. 3, pp. 611–35; the reference here is to p. 622. The order provides one more

The fact that more than one stamp survives, and that they have been most carefully and clearly franked (as those illustrated show), is rather surprising.

A Rowling 8 Annas postage stamp franked with the postal cancellation "Ankole No 20 98" (20th November 1898)

Very few letters would have been sent by members of a reconnaissance party led by Macallister in November, and it has been suggested that he cancelled a considerable number without them being genuinely sent through the post. It does *not* seem that the case against Macallister has been really proved, especially as these 'stamps' were then of little value after use, but if they were cancelled to order there is no certainty that this was done on the date which appears on the stamp. It could have been done later and any covers may not have actually passed though the postal system.

However, what matters here is whether the 20th November 1898 is a genuine date at all. If Macallister was responsible for setting the hand stamp, either genuinely at the time or cancelling to order later, he would presumably have chosen a realistic date, and so the existence of such cancellations would seem to support the view that his preliminary visit to Ankole occurred in this month. If he was in Ankole on the 20th November he would still have had time to get back to Kampala or Entebbe before setting out again for Mbarara on the 2nd December. If he had just completed a rapid *safari* it would account for the rather leisurely progress, which he made, not reaching Mbarara until the 18th.

It has also been pointed out that as "the Uganda hand stamps would have been supplied to Kampala and issued from there, could it be that the responsible official tried his hand out

evidence that it was intended to set up a British Administration in Nkore long before this was achieved.

on some sheets of Rowling stamps, with all the various hand stamps?[284] As the Rowling issues were still valid this would seem to be an eccentric, if not criminal, waste – especially on values of 8 annas and 1 rupee!

It does not seem that Uganda hand stamps were being used much before the beginning of November 1898, the Kampala one apparently being the first,[285] and we have already noted that Macallister was there at the beginning of the month. Since November 1898 is the most likely of the possibilities, and with the confirmatory evidence of these Rowling stamps, the indications are that Macallister's initial visit to the *Omugabe* at Rushasha did take place during that month.

While it must be granted that the 1898 Ankole frankings may not be genuine at all, the fact that stamps exist bearing dates in November of that year and the following January is at least coincidental and must be remarked in the face of known British activity in the area at the time. With Macallister's apparent interest in philately and the known use of the Ankole hand stamps legitimately in early January 1899, it is most likely that he was responsible for the Rowling stamps which bear the 'Ankole No 20 98' franking, and that these give a precise date to his initial visit, whether they were done at that time, or 'forged' later.

Note

I am most grateful to the late Roy Hart Dunstan (1917–2006) who first introduced me to the Macallister covers and generously gave me a couple of the Rowling stamps. He amassed an important collection of such material, which was auctioned in 1985. An article in *The Independ-*

---

[284] Personal communication from Mr R. Dunstan, 7th June 1976; though he does not consider this likely.

[285] Flood, Dr W.E., 'The Early Cancellations of East Africa and Uganda', *South African Philatelist*, February 1956: "Cancelling date stamps were introduced in 1898. Kampala was the first office to use a date stamp: the date has been variously recorded as 'August' and autumn, but my earliest copy is November 1st."

ent, Saturday, 18 August 2007 gives some details about him. In his youth he was asked to leave Sutton Valence School after a series of boisterous escapades, and went on to Dulwich College, where he became a Prefect and Captain of Athletics. From King's College Hospital he qualified as a dentist. His other interests, besides philately, included being Mayor of Warminster, and Chamberlain of the *Commarderie* of Great Britain of the International Order of Anysetiers, the guild of producers and traders in aniseed founded in France in the 13th Century, and which now opens its ranks to lovers of anis, gastronomy and convivial company.

APPENDIX C

THE JOURNEY OF CUNNINGHAM
THROUGH ANKOLE IN 1894

On 25th July Major G. G. Cunningham left Port Alice (Entebbe) with a force of fifty-seven troops of the Uganda Rifles and sixty-five Swahili porters. His orders were to march through Buddu, as a show of strength, and relieve Mr J. P. Wilson who was surrounded by "hostile natives" at Marongo on the Ankole border.[286] Wilson had been on his way to make a treaty with Ntare, the *Omugabe* of Nkore, before taking charge of Toro district. Cunningham was to assist Wilson in any way necessary and take over acting as envoy to Ntare. As it turned out he felt his first task was to escort Wilson as far as Fort George at Katwe, the administrative station in Usongora, and then to tackle the question of negotiating with Ntare afterwards.

The name of his territory (Nkore) became anglicised as Ankole, and this spelling has persisted under British and later Administrations in describing the whole of the Ankole District. At this time of early encounter both terms were variously used, but for consistency here Ankole will be used from now on, though until 1898 Nkore is more accurate.

A good deal of uncertainty seems to exist about the route, which was taken on this expedition. As a European traveller Cunningham undoubtedly covered considerable new ground on this occasion. An attempt is made to recognise this on the *Atlas of Uganda* map of 'Early Travels',[287]

---

[286] Colvile, H. E., *op. cit.* pp. 287–290. Colonel Colvile quotes the letter he received (as Commissioner) from J. P. Wilson, dated Marongo, 17th July 1894, ESA file A/2/2.

[287] Early travels, *Atlas of Uganda,* first edition, (1962), p. 73, second edition, (1967), p. 73

though as B. W. Langlands says this route is "only roughly mapped."[288] Published references to Cunningham's presence in Ankole are extremely few.[289] There is for instance no reference to Cunningham's traverse in Lukyn Williams article on explorers' routes through Ankole[290] nor in the more recent follow up of this by Ntare pupils.[291] Moreover, the 1900 map of Uganda by J. R. L. Macdonald shows numerous routes through Ankole taken later by Macallister, but the name Cunningham does not appear,[292] and undoubtedly it is to this map that the more generous allocation of new Ankole routes to Macallister must be attributed. This is at the expense of Cunningham (especially with reference to the Mbarara-Koki route) on the *Atlas of Uganda* map.[293] This only suggests the possibility of a pioneering route by Cunningham westwards from Masaka through Lyantonde to Mbarara, and thence north-west to join up with the route taken by the botanist G. F. Scott Elliot earlier in the same year.

---

[288] Langlands, B. W., 'Early travellers in Uganda'. *UJ*, 26, 1962, p. 64.

[289] The inclusion of Cunningham's name on the *Atlas* map depends only upon a brief reference to the establishment of British administration in the district in Ingham, K., *The making of modern Uganda*, (1958), p. 65.

[290] Lukyn Williams, F., 'Early explorers in Ankole', *UJ*, 2/3, (1935), pp. 196–248. However, there is a brief account in his article on Mbaguta, *op. cit.* (1946). This is based on Parliamentary Paper, Africa, no. 7 (1895), no. 53.

[291] Ntare School History Society, 'The journey of Stanley through Ankole in 1889'. *UJ*, **29**, (1965), pp. 185–192.

[292] *Map* of *Uganda*, J. R. L. Macdonald, Intelligence Division, War Office, 1900, (1 inch to 10 miles). The reason for the full treatment given to Macallister's activities by Macdonald was that the former had drawn a map of the District of Ankole, which was forwarded from Entebbe to London on the 26th April 1900 (Public Record Office in London: FO. 2/298, no. 99). Macallister very property marked his map with the 'roads traversed in 1899 and 1900' and Macdonald incorporated this information onto his map. Macallister's 'Sketch Map of Ankole District' (1 inch to 10 miles) will be found in the map room P.R.O., under MPK. 122, C.7095.

[293] Personal communication from B. W. Langlands.

Research at the Entebbe Secretariat Archives, however, reveals that Cunningham's own account survives and the basis of this record of early travels in Ankole requires substantial revision. Two records of Cunningham's work in Ankole exist. Firstly there is his report to the Commissioner, Colonel Colvile,[294] and then an attachment to it, "Description of the Country Passed through by the Ankole expedition 1894, via King Ntale's Capital."[295] A 'road chart' was supposed to have accompanied the latter, but this has not been found.

Having crossed the river Katonga on 30th July 1894, Cunningham passed through Buddu in a fairly leisurely fashion to reach Marongo on 5th August. Here he discovered that Wilson's enemies were the *Futabangi* (Bhang smokers). He spent a day in taking over command of the expedition. Incidentally Wilson felt that his reputation was likely to suffer as a result of not having succeeded in his mission to Ntare. On the other hand Cunningham was in no doubt about success and reported to Colvile "I leave here tomorrow (7th August) for Busozi (Nabushozi) awaiting a reply from Ntale. If necessary I will escort Mr. Wilson to Fort George and then proceed to Ntale's."[296]

Continuing on to Kabula on 7th August, he spent a day exacting payment for plundered trade goods. He then passed through Nabushozi to Romohoro (Rwomuhoro) where "some messengers arrived from Ntali with sheep, salaams, and a message to say he hoped to see me on my return journey."[297] The party reached Bwera in Mitoma on 13th August; Kitete (marked on Scott Elliot's map) on 15th; Kichwamba (in Bun-

---

[294] Cunningham, G. G., 'The report of the Ankole Expedition', Cunningham to Commissioner, Port Alice, 24th September 1894. ESA, A/2/3: referred to subsequently as Report no.1.

[295] Cunningham, G. G, 'Description of the country passed through by the Ankole. Expedition 1894, via King Ntale's capital.' ESA, A/2/2, 24 September 1894; subsequently referred to as Report no.2. He also wrote two letters *en route* (i) from Marongo dated the 6 August (ii) from Kazinga ferry dated 21st August. Both are in file A/2/2.

[296] Cunningham, Report no. 1, *op. cit.*

[297] Cunningham, Report no. 2, *op. cit.*

yaruguru) on 17th; and Fort George on 19th. Thus on the outward journey Cunningham seems to have followed Lugard's route of 1891 fairly closely, and certainly not to have gone to Ntare direct.

After arriving at Fort George, Wilson wrote to Colvile on 21st August "I will go to Kasagama's shortly. ... I will build a new station on the sight [*sic*] of the one which was burned down on the evacuation of Toro."[298]

Having successfully assisted Wilson to his place of duty, Cunningham now turned his attention to the matter of Ntare. Losing no time, he began the journey south on 21st August, crossing the channel by the ferry at Kazinga. Here he stayed the night and wrote his second letter to Colvile. The chief of the area, Kaihura, lent two guides, both of whom deserted within two days. At first the path across the plain by which they had come was followed to Kichwamba on the escarpment. Before arriving there, however, the path "which diverges to the south"[299] was taken, and thereafter new ground was broken for a European traverse through Ankole. It would seem that Kaihura's guides led the party during most of 22nd and 23rd. The report gives the following description of this part of the journey:

> Then comes two days of very hilly country, though the gradients of the paths are not excessively steep. The country from Rusoze to Igara is well timbered, but from the latter place to Ntengo none, though there are several streams and marshes on the road.

From this it would seem that Cunningham skirted the crater area of the escarpment and avoided the dense Maramagambo forest, keeping to the lower hills. Both the 1900 map (Macdonald's) and a 1910 Ankole[300] district map give Lusozi (Rusoze) as another name for Bunyaruguru.[301]

---

[298]   J. P. Wilson to Commissioner, Kazinga ferry, 21st August 1894. ESA, file A/2/2.

[299]   Quotations hereafter, until otherwise stated, are from Report no. 2, *op. cit.*

[300]   Lands and Surveys Archives, Entebbe; Miscellaneous no. 76. Sketch map of Ankole District, 1910 (scale 1 inch to 10 miles).

[301]   Frequently it appears that Cunningham was told the name of an 'area'

The expedition passed from Rusoze to Igara on 23th August through well-timbered country. Scott Elliot[302] marks Igara as a place at a height of 4,700 feet, probably in the region of the present factory at Kitozho. The next day was spent in crossing treeless country but with "several streams and marshes on the road", to reach Ntengo (Elliot's Nengo; and Enego on current maps still in Igara).

Cunningham takes up the story for 25th August. "The fourth day's march lies along a splendid road, leading to the very large village of Sima, over undulating country, but no timber." Again Scott Elliot indicates such a place roughly in the vicinity of Kigarama in Sheema. The party then entered a vast undulating plain with here and there solitary cone-shaped hills. This plain is surrounded by hills on all sides, the Ruampara range bounding it on the south. "It appears fertile, with numerous villages dotted about, but devoid of timber." Even today this would still be a very fair description of the country seen on the road towards Mbarara from Itendero or Masheruka. "Across the middle of the plain flows a marsh called Iksheragenyi, which appears to be the upper part of the river Rwizi." From any modern map of Ankole it is clear that this is describing the Kooga Swamp. The 1: 50,000 Kabwohe sheet marks a rise on the east side of this swamp, which is two miles northwest of Kashaka Hill, and it bears the name Kichuragenyi. If Cunningham crossed the Kooga near this point, he might well have been told this name (though his spelling of it was his own), and so thought that the whole swamp was called by that name.

On 26th August camp was made at Ruampoko. Of this place the report states that,

Here an effort was made to induce us to take a northern

---

when enquiring for the name of a particular 'place'. Thus as well as Rusoze, he used present county names Igara, Sima (Sheema) and Kasari (Kashari) as though they were particular places.

302   Elliot, G. F, Scott. *op. cit.* has a map of East Africa (for part of which, see above p.125). This marks what must have been Cunningham's route, though it is not named as such, and gives the place-names Igara, Nengo, Sima, Nsara, Ntali, but the location of the last named is clearly erroneous.

road towards Marongo, in the hope of getting us away from the neighbourhood of Ntali's. It was quite evident from the general scare that we had arrived close to the latter's capital. The guides who brought us to Ruampoko fled without even waiting for the customary present of cloth.[303]

The crossing of the Kooga near Kichuragenyi also fits in with the camp at Ruampoko, as Rwempongo is about one mile north of Kashaka Hill, and Ntare's capital was only about twelve miles away.

> Here (at Ruampoko) the messenger who came to Entebbe turned up, accompanied by another ambassador from Ntali and a present of sheep, sent to ask what I had come for. I replied 'at his invitation to make a treaty', and because he had told you (i.e. Colvile) Ntali wanted a European to come. Hereupon the second envoy exclaimed that Ntali had never given such instructions to the other messenger. I declined to accept this, saying Ntali had sent for us, and I must see him. He went off to see the King, and returned in the evening with an ox, saying he had instructions to ask us to go to Marongo, where I should hear from the King, and affirming that the latter had left his village, and taken refuge in the mountains, as he would on no account see a white man. I refused. He then said he would take us next day to a place conveniently near to Ntali's from where negotiations could be conducted.

Next day (27th August) the march began at 6 a.m. and "the guide took us by a road north into what seemed a sterile and waterless country." North of Rwempongo lies a grassy, rather hilly region with the Kooga swamp away to the west. Bearing in mind that it was August when the main dry season is usually at its climax, with the grass burnt brown and a general air of desolation, this description will cause no surprise, especially when the party had come down from the higher, better watered country and passed through the very swampy area of Sheema.

Cunningham rapidly came to the conclusion that he was being deceived, and turned back.

> After numerous stoppages I declined to go further. The

---

[303] This and the following quotations are taken from Report no. 1, *op. cit.*, unless otherwise stated.

messengers went off to get fresh orders, and we marched across country back to the main road to Ntali's, halting at 9 a.m. at Kasari.

In fact it looks as if this day's march was entirely futile as "Kasari" was none other than the name given to Kashaka Hill. Here Cunningham was crossing the route, which Stanley took when travelling south through Ankole in 1889.[304]

On 28th August another start was made with a similar result, the messenger

trying to take us north, while I steered east, and after two hours march we arrived in sight of Ntali's village. Here I halted at a place called Kitabwenda, which we were told later was only one and half hours

from Ntare's. As both Ishanya (site of the present Stock Farm) and Ruharo (where St. James' Cathedral stands) are modern names derived from *Luganda*, Kitabwenda might well have been either of these places. The former is likely as it would not have been possible to get much further east in a two hours march.

In his 'Description of the Country', Cunningham says that "Ntali's village is situated at the extreme southeast corner of this plain at the foot of a five peaked hill named Kakiika." Rather surprisingly he does not say that it was also south of the Ruizi, although Colvile is quite definite on this point.[305] The explanation given by the Ntare School History Society for a similar omission by Stanley may well be true of Cunningham also: it is simply that in the dry season crossing the Ruizi provided no particular obstacle, and so it was not mentioned.[306]

Many months of scanning the skyline in and around the Mbarara area convinces me that there is only one hill, which could be so described. Certainly Cunningham cannot have been referring to the well-known hill, Kakiika, a little to the

---

[304] Lukyn Williams, *op. cit.* 2/3 (1935) speaks of Kashari, p. 200, "This place is the same as the present (Kashaka)" and the Ntare School group also agreed with this, *op. cit.*, p. 190.

[305] Colvile, *op. cit.*, p. 110.

[306] Ntare School, *op. cit.* p. 190; for another possibility see above note 110.

north of the town. Even with the adjoining hill this cannot be regarded as five-peaked, and of course *it is* north of the river. On the other hand there is a rather distinctive hill which from certain directions appears to be five-peaked, lying just across the river to the south of Bishop Stuart Teacher Training College at Kakoba. This is now marked as Kyarwanshashura although earlier maps called it Bihunya, the name now given to the longer adjoining hill. Locally, however, Kyarwansashura (the place of being paid back) is known at present as Rwenkobe (the mountain of apes). Kakiika (the smooth place) is also well-known locally, besides the hill already mentioned, for example, the site on which Ntare school now stands was previously known by that name.

Thus there seems to be little reason why Cunningham should not have been told that Ntare's capital was at the foot of Kakiika, but meaning, Kyarwanshashura. Below the hill is an area now called Katete and here Ntare certainly had a Kraal. Another factor indicating the same conclusion is the comment that "immediately behind his village is a pass through the hills leading towards the Ruampara mountains." When looking between Kyarwanshashura and Bihunya this is exactly the impression one gets, although strictly speaking what one sees is the Gayaza ridge in Isingiro, which is a continuation of the Ruampara hills. Having arrived at this conclusion it was learnt locally that

> the *Omugabe* Ntare established his place at Katete beyond the Ruizi river opposite Kakoba in 1894. Then while at Katete the *Omugabe* ordered Mbaguta to sign on his behalf the treaty with Major Cunningham.[307]

---

[307] From information supplied by Mr A. G. Katate, personal communication. Lukyn Williams, *op. cit.* (1946), p. 128 states that Ntare's "was situated at this time at Kaigoshora in Kashari county." This would not seem to be correct, and it is probably explained by the fact that Ntare was soon to be chased "up to the north-eastern border with Buganda" by invasion from Rwanda. (Karugire, *op. cit.*, [1971] pp. 229–230). He died at Kaigoshora less than a year after Cunningham's Journey. Kaigoshora is about ten miles north of Mbarara and does not fit Cunningham's account at several points.

To return to the vicissitudes of the journey, Cunningham was at Kitabwenda on 28th August, and here

> numerous messengers arrived from the King, begging us to
> proceed to Marongo, where I should hear from him. I
> replied that the King must send some person of note as his
> representative.

Unable to get the European to go away and clearly unwilling
to attack him, Ntare took some time to act. Not until the following afternoon does Cunningham continue this story.

> At 4 p.m. (29th August) the Katikiro Magota (Mbaguta) ar-
> rived with full powers (he said). He signed the treaty for the
> King, requested that a black man might be sent in future as
> your representative as Ntali would not see a European.
>
> Next day (30th August) we marched at 6 a.m. and af-
> ter one and half hours arrived at Ntali's – a mere village.
> His house is square and high, surrounded by eight other
> huts of the usual beehive pattern, the whole in an enclo-
> sure.

However, Ntare himself had retired through the pass between the hills "whilst about 500 of his spearman lined the
pass and neighbouring hills as we approached."

Thus it took Cunningham's party ten days to travel from
Fort George to Ntare's but only some of these were effective
full day marches. The 22nd–26th were fairly full days, but
the travelling done on the 27th, 28th and 30th could have
been accomplished on one normal day's march. The 29th
was spent at Kitabwenda. Only six or seven were effective
marching days. A few years later after the setting up of the
European administration in Ankole, the journey from
Kazinga to Mbarara was reckoned as a six-day one totalling
thirty and half hours marching, so that Cunningham's time
was quite consistent.[308]

There was no point in lingering at the deserted capital so
"the march was resumed, the guides again taking us north."
Presumably the Ruizi was crossed immediately and then

> the country becomes hilly and wooded though the road is

---

[308] Woodward, E.M. *Précis* of *information concerning The Uganda
Protectorate,* Intelligence Division, War Office, H.M.S.O., 1902,
Route 14 Mbarara-Kazinga (Alternative route), p. 124.

level, leading through the hills by a pass, along the side of a valley into a small wooded plain, after which the hills narrow again, forming a short pass, then, opening out again into another small wooded plain.

The precise route here is hard to follow, especially as a wooded plain then might by now have been cleared, but he must have passed to the west of Rwemigina (5154 feet) and probably Kaburangira and Rwagaaju as well, so as to take the pass through which the present Masaka road goes at about 7 miles. Hereafter details are much more vague, but Cunningham was heading for the capital of Kamswaga, King of Koki, which he did not reach until 5th September complaining that the northern route taken by his guides proved to be two days longer than a "direct road from Ntali's to Kamuswaga's."[309] Clearly he passed the northern end of Lake Kachira, somewhere near Lyantonde, and then turned south until he reached Kamuswaga's village "which is situated a day's march from the south of Lake Kachera, close to a small lake called Rikondo." (Presumably this meant Lake Kijanebalola).

Enough has now been said to show that Cunningham crossed Ankole along a route not previously taken by a British traveller and that this can be traced with some accuracy. Cunningham's own opinion was that "on the return journey we took a road which led to Ntali's village, which I think has never before been visited by a European. It is certainly marked wrong on all the maps I have seen." Colvile shared this opinion describing "Ntali's town as a spot which I believe, no European had before succeeded in reaching."[310]

Colvile was undoubtedly right, and Cunningham certainly was the first European to travel from the Mbarara area across to Koki in the way he did. However in his journey from Katwe he had been anticipated in general by nearly a year. We have already observed that Captain Langheld of the German Imperial Army, having travelled through Karagwe and Mpororo to Fort George, which he found aban-

---

[309]   Report no. 2, *op. cit.*

[310]   Colvile, *op. cit.*, p. 293.

doned and burnt, decided to return to Bukoba by the quickest way through Ankole. In doing so he arrived within four
fours of Ntare's capital on 12th September 1893. Suspicious
of his intentions, the *Omugabe's* men asked him to move
further off to Birere (five miles south of Mbarara) on the
following day. It was here there that the tragic encounter
occurred causing Langheld to re-enter Karagwe as quickly
as possible.[311]

Details of Langheld's route are no clearer to me than
this: that he, too obviously made his way from Katwe to the
Mbarara area. In so doing he must have traversed similar
country to that crossed by the British expedition, and therefore the *Atlas of Uganda* map of early travels again needs
correcting to indicate this journey.[312]

At all events Cunningham clearly showed considerable
initiative and determination in reaching Ntare's capital. In
many ways he seems typical of the more able British military officer of the time. Born in 1862 into a soldiering family, George Glencairn Cunningham received his education at
Wellington College and Sandhurst. Writing of Wellington a
decade later Mr G. F. H. Berkeley described it as, "an un-
commonly good place during these years ... a splendid insti-
tution for the Nation and for the Empire," aiming "to turn
out a hardy and dashing breed of young officers."[313]

Cunningham seems to fit this description well enough,
and distinguished himself in an unusual amount of active

---

[311]   Gray, *op. cit.*, gives details of Langheld's activity as drawn from W.
        Langheld, *op. cit.* p. 164. A copy of this has been deposited in the
        Royal Commonwealth Society Library. I am most grateful to the
        Librarian and to Mr A. T. Matson, literary executor, for permission to
        quote from page 59 of this work. His fight is described above in
        Chapter 2.

[312]   In compiling the *Atlas* map the omission of Langheld's Journey was
        known (cf. Langlands, *op. cit.*, p. 62), though it was mistakenly
        believed that the passage through south Ankole had taken place in
        early 1892, not 1893. It was not, however, realised that Langheld got
        as far as Fort George. Personal communication from B. W. Langlands.

[313]   Berkeley, G. F. H., *My recollections of Wellington College*, pp. 21–23,
        quoted in, Newsome, D., *Godliness and good learning*, p. 201.

service for those days. Indeed, having been commissioned into the Duke of Cornwall's Light Infantry in 1881, the next twenty years were packed with adventure. He went at once to the battle-fields of Egypt in support of the Government, took part in a number of engagements, was twice wounded at the battle of Kassassin prior to a more major action at Tel-el-Kebir, mentioned in despatches, and awarded the 5th class of the Order of the *Medjidieh.* Then followed five years in the Sudan, first with the Nile Expedition of 1884–1885, and then attached to the Egyptian Army serving with the Sudan Frontier Field Force until 1889, when he was promoted Captain and Brevet Major in the Derby Regiment. He also received a second Ottoman decoration, the 4th class of the Order of *Osmanieh.*

A quieter period followed before his service in Uganda from 19th January 1894 to 26th August 1896, officially in civil employ but seeing plenty of action. After leading the peaceful Ankole Expedition as it was called, he went on to command the warlike expeditions into Unyoro in 1895, where he was again wounded and mentioned in despatches, and Nandi in 1895–1896. For that he received the Distinguished Service Order (D.S.O.) in recognition of "recent operations against slave-trading Arabs in the Uganda Protectorate."[314] Two years in West Africa ensued, firstly as a Brevet Lieut.-Colonel on the Niger, with another mention in despatches, before serving in Sierra Leone until 1899, with another mention and Brevet of Colonel.

The South Africa war broke out in the same year and for two years there he held the local of Brigadier-General to command a Brigade,[315] and was made a Companion of the Order of the Bath (C.B.),[316] with yet another mention. At the end of the war he married, and retired as a Colonel in the Royal Scots in 1909, only to be recalled for the First World War. He commanded of the Plymouth General Reserve and

---

[314]   *The London Gazette*, 3rd November 1896.

[315]   *Ibid*, 11th September 1900, but effective from 13th July, eleven days before his thirty-eighth birthday, though still only a substantive Major.

[316]   *Ibid*, 19th April 1901.

then served as Base Commandant at Brest from 1917–1919. For this last appointment he was awarded the C.B.E. and the French made him a Commander of the *Legion d'Honneur*. In 1919 he finally retired as a Brigadier General.

In later life his public service continued in a different form as Mayor of Hythe in Kent, where he lived in retirement.[317] He died three days before his 81st birthday on 21st July 1943, in the midst of another World War. Being aware of the unusual nature of the fifteen Orders and medals he had received, he bequeathed replicas of them to the 1st Battalions of both The Sherwood Foresters into which The Derby Regiment had been absorbed, and The Royal Scots, which presumably he had commanded after finally returning from Africa. Described as a "unique collection", the originals were sold at auction by Dix, Noonan, Webb, of Mayfair for £8,500 in 2003.[318]

This was the man then who made the last European attempt to deal directly with Ntare. It cannot be imagined that this *Omugabe* would ever have changed his mind in order to deal face to face with a white man. However, less than a year after Cunningham left Ankole Ntare was dead, but much more was now known about his country. The value of this journey would be proved when new possibilities opened up once a successor was established in the leadership. Therefore, it must be reckoned to have had a great deal of bearing on events that led to the founding of Mbarara four years later.

---

[317] *Who Was Who 1941–50*, London (1952).

[318] For the award of the *Legion d'Honneur*, see *The London Gazette*, 18th July 1919; for the bequest of replicas, see *The Nottingham Evening Post*, 10th November 1943, p.1; all his original Orders and medals were included as Lot 436 when Dix, Noonan, Webb held their auction on 2nd July 2003.

MAP 6 CUNNINGHAM'S JOURNEY

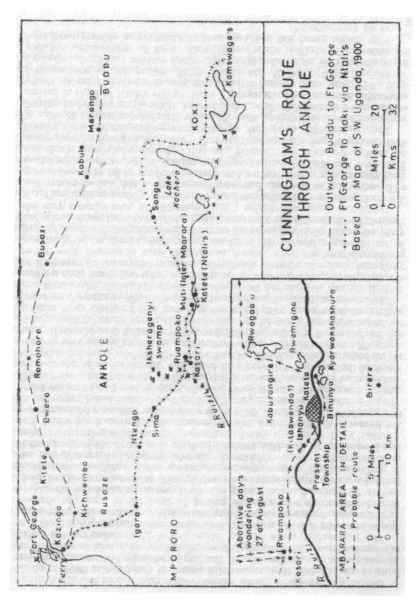

The original can be found in *UJ* (1973) *op. cit.* p. 57.

APPENDIX D

A FEW PERSONAL RECOLLECTIONS OF MBARARA
BY AN APPRECIATIVE *MUZUNGU*

These random comments are not any necessary part of this book. Please ignore them if you will, though some other memories have already been recorded in previous comments here, see under 'Family' in the Index.

Our family arrived in Mbarara by Government taxi. When it stopped outside the Office at Ntare School, I got out to announce our coming. The person I met with was the Bursar. After greetings, and chatting to him for some time, he paid me the considerable compliment that I had been in Africa before. I had not said so, though it was true, and did not know that it was obvious. (Also, I had worked with "colonial troops".)

So here at once were two issues, colour and empire. They are also now raised in this study of Mbarara. Dr Karugire introduced the problem of colour in describing Europeans as "red". Colour is a matter best dealt with humorously for none of us has any control over it.

Long ago I shared a flat in Leeds with a Nigerian medical student who is now Dr A. O. B. Olugbile. Later we would come to Uganda only after an appointment in Northern Nigeria had suddenly fallen through. 'Dapo had the right approach when he was in a coloured minority, having great fun in teasing us "white" people. In one example, he delighted to say that things were "Flesh coloured." When everyone else was thinking light, he was describing something far richer.

When newly come to Mbarara, our little son, aged three, very soon asked us, with nothing but a simple curiosity, "When will I go black?" Also I found it amusing that while some of us were trying to get browner, others were using Ambi cream to attempt the opposite effect.

Again, when my wife, Jean, first faced a class of forty bright Ntare pupils, she asked for patience as she struggled with the names, calling out each in turn. In one case she was told in all seriousness, "He is the black one, madam." So indeed were the Nilotics from the north, in contrast to the various browns of the *Bantu*. We both soon learnt to distinguish for ourselves, but it cut both ways. During the emergency in 1972, when we were briefly in Kampala, a group of Japanese tourists were arrested because it was thought they were British.

Perhaps it was about that time that our daughter, then no more than four, wanted to bring a friend home from the *Boma* School for tea. Asking how we should recognise the friend, we were told that she was the one with the red shoes. Josephine turned out to be a stunningly beautiful little girl and very dark. Rightly, none of that had entered into the very apt description given by infant wisdom.

On our way home the ship stayed over night in Durban. We had a family walk along the promenade. Passing signs showing on either side, *Blancs* and *Ni-Blancs*, our seven year old son asked the meaning. When told of *Apartheid*, he replied after his experience of four years at the Mbarara *Boma*, "That's stupid!" Humour or dismissal is the way to treat any problems arising from our skins or race.

It would be invidious to name any of those we taught at Ntare. How could we name one and not another? We have happy memories of so many, and thrill at the occasional news of one or two. There were no real disciplinary problems in class. Pupils were so keen to learn, knew that others had made sacrifices for them to have the opportunity, and that this was the key to their future. All the classrooms were single-storey with open windows. Only twice did those I was teaching all jump up and leap out of them. Being on a fault-line, there was once a substantial earth tremor and the building began to shake. The second time a small aircraft flew overhead. Such an event was almost unknown, and quite outside the experience of many. Thus on both occasions their strange behaviour was entirely justified.

Then there was empire. I have said before that this seems to have been a necessary but passing interlude, a bridge to pass over to something new. Some understood this from the start. There was Bishop Tucker (CMS) with his wonderful vision of the Native Anglican Church, conceived so early in his time and long ago achieved.

There were some who saw it as an opportunity. What a privilege to have known Mr Mbide, who supplied us with pasteurised milk. In the 1930s he had got to know the Government Vet in Ankole who was British. He spoke of him with great warmth and respect, having had the wit to learn much from him. Now years later here he was very successful, with his herd of exotic cattle somewhere in the bush. We heard rumours of his wonderful house. In those days the *muzungu* pecking order in Mbarara was headed by the Bank Manager. We were asked to dinner once, and having satisfied the suspicions of the *askari* or night-watchman (we knew of no one else who had one), went into the opulence of this mansion with its parquet floors. Any others at best were concrete. We heard that Mr Mbide aspired to have a house built just like that far out in the countryside. One day we were invited to his home, and there was the house – with its parquet floors!

Another such was William Ndahuchere of happy memory. Old Ntarean after its founding in colonial days, he was the first from the school to be trained at Sandhurst. Commanding a battalion of the Uganda army at the time of the military coup, Amin saw such able and well trained officers as a threat and soon had him retired. The Colonel returned to his native Ankole and burst on the local scene, at least in our experience. We were invited to a thanksgiving service in the Cathedral at Ruharo, This was to give praise to God for his safe return from the military and there I met him for the first time. He looked an impressive leader of men, with his cheerful out-going personality and equally notable military moustache. His accompanying wife was a Princess of Toro (presumably Elizabeth's sister).

I took to him at once and asked him what he was going to do now. He replied with a grin, "Get my hands dirty!" and he opened his palms. This sounded extraordinary. The last thing our generation of Ntareans wanted to do was to work the land like Mr Mbide, still less like many fathers in their *shambas*. The young were for the professions and the high places. Anyway, here was an able, intelligent man, intent on working the land in his own way. For some of the results of this endeavour, see note 166.

I met him once or twice later, when he came into Mbarara in his Landrover. Wisely, in the back were some powerful dogs. Despite such precautions, later I was greatly saddened to hear that Amin's henchmen had got him in the end.

So it is a pleasure, and sometimes a sorrow, to remember many others among the local people we knew in Mbarara. In our day most still had pictures of the Queen in their houses. It was then the age of radio rather than television. Throughout our years there was a constant flow of anti-British, anti-Imperial propaganda over the air-waves and in the newspapers. This seemed not to have had the slightest effect on Mbarara people, who always treated us with kindness and expressed pleasure at our presence among them. Their attitude towards us to the end remained open, cheerful and positive, and it was the same elsewhere.

Most notably for me there was the warm fellowship of the Church of Uganda; the welcome from Bishop Shalita who was delighted to license me; the invitation from the Dean to lead the English speaking services, first in St James's Cathedral and then at All Saints, Mbarara when it was finally built; the fellowship of other clergy like Eli Muhoozi (soon to be Archdeacon) and Yoramu Bamunoba (soon to be a Bishop); the evocative atmosphere of Clayton's old roofless church at Kamukuzi, with its little graveyard. All of us "one in Christ Jesus."

Then, still in Obote's day, there was an Election. I was chatting to the owner of a shop in town. He asked me how I had voted. Unlike in Britain now, though resident (and from the Commonwealth) I had no vote. Naturally in return I asked him the same question. He had not voted, indeed could not. Apparently then one's vote was cast by lining up outside the local offices of either the Democratic Party (dubbed "Dependents of the Pope") or the Uganda People's Congress ("United Protestants of Canterbury"). Thus politics tended to divide along denominational lines. The shopkeeper believed that if he were to be seen publicly in one queue or the other, he would offend certain of his customers, and so lose them. For me, this was a new slant on the many problems of democracy.

Then there were the practical skills we learnt in Mbarara. There is only room to pass on the two most pressing tips. If you want to prevent an ant *safari* entering your home, pour old sump oil at the base of the outside walls, especially at any doorways; if you want to drive the bats from infesting your roof and avoid the inconvenience of their messy dropping, bring motor-bikes into the building and 'rev' them up to the loudest extent. Bats do not like it, and will leave you in sole possession.[319]

We have discussed translation work in Chapter Nine. I found myself engaged in a different kind. The 1960s were already a day of concern about the need to revise the King James *Authorised Version* of the Bible into modern English. The *Revised Stand Version* already existed by then. I encountered a different problem with the *Book of Common Prayer of 1662*. This was still standard in Britain, but Ankole had it right up-to-date in *Runyankore-Rukiga*. Ntare was intentionally an English speaking environment, and I was troubled by using the *BCP* in services there. Having learnt English, there was now a need to know sixteenth century vocabulary. Therefore in 1970 I produced the *Ntare Prayer Book* for services on Sunday, and *Ntare Daily Prayer*, for use in our short daily morning worship, often led by boys. These were simple publications, run off cyclostyled at school, bound up by a local Asian and with a printed cover. All services were voluntary and increasingly well attended as the political situation worsened and many embraced the living faith of their parents.

Then, on matters of colonialism, what can be said of the lingeringly named Order of the British Empire? Kahaya II and Mbaguta, king and minister, had both been Members (M.B.E.), as were Mr Kamugungunu and Canon Buningwire, among others. Mr Z. C. K. Mungonya was a Commander (C.B.E.). I was fortunate to have known the last three. I am not aware of any British colonial officials in Ankole being so honoured, though I did know three then in Mbarara who were Officers (O.B.E.)

Some might find it strange that so many of the old "colonialists" were retained to go on working for the newly independent African regimes. In Mbarara there was William

---

[319] I have done my best to circulate this second tip, see letter to *The Times*, 23rd July 2014.

Machar Crichton, an Aberdonian known as Will, the founding Headmaster of Ntare School. After long years in the Sudan he had seen the country gain independence and came on to Uganda. He saw the same achievement there and for years afterwards continued to make a great contribution to the advancement of education.

Then there was the Cornishman, Thomas Frederick Ellis, known as Tom. He had been a Major in the Indian Army, and now was fulfilling a key role as District Agricultural Officer in Ankole.

Most notable of all there was Algernon Charles Stanley-Smith. "Doctor Algy" was the son of one of "the Cambridge Seven" missionaries who was killed in the Boxer Rebellion, in China in 1900. Having won the Military Cross as a young medical officer on the Western Front early in the First World War, he was posted to Uganda. Soon afterwards he transferred to the Church Missionary Society and served the people of western Uganda and Rwanda for the next sixty years. As a doctor he eradicated two endemic diseases from the area and was largely responsible for translating the Bible into two of the vernaculars, one of them *Runyankore-Rukiga.*

With his wife Zoe, this octogenarian couple were universally loved and respected, as much by the local population as by expatriates, however godless they might be – so much for the evil missionary of contemporary 'political correctness'. Be that as it may, these three men could all be viewed askance as having been decorated (O.B.E.), and as Imperial agents as our radios taught us. On the contrary, despite the name, their recognition by the Queen was not for services to the Empire, but for their long years of devotion to the welfare of the people among whom they worked so hard.

So, with this in mind, let us now return to this place whose foundation we are celebrating. In 1973, a friend there returned briefly to visit her family in a remote part of the Ankole. It was a time of great internal repression, with many deaths. She had told her grandfather that there was trouble in Mbarara. His reassuring answer caused us great amusement at the time, when she told it to us all. "Don't worry, my dear, King George will never allow it." Was this really a foible of age, or had not news of his death, let alone of Independence, yet reached the furthest parts?

Of course, it is true that imperial government is an "unnatural" rule. Of course, the local population have no opportunity of exercising the ultimate power. Of course outside influences were strong. For most of us in Britain in a new century these things are somewhat academic. We do not have power here; influences that we do not like too often prevail over our comfort of mind.

Nevertheless, what matters to most of us is that we live in security, with law and order properly maintained, with the opportunity to be educated, to choose a reasonable vocation and pursue it, hopeful that our children may have as good, or better opportunities than we had, and within the law to live as we choose. All those same opportunities came to be provided by the Colonial Administration, and those who spent their lives in its service were the agents, handing over to their African successors who have the self same obligation. It was the Mayor of Lagos who wisely said in 1960, when his country became independent, that he hoped the new independence would be better than the old, a very proper aspiration, a longing and a hope.

Very sadly for us, a thick veiled dropped when we left Uganda. It was not safe to keep in touch with Ugandan friends for the arrival of a British airmail might lead to allegations of disloyalty, even of treason. We returned to Scotland for the next twenty years, far removed from the international mecca of London. Shortly before we did leave Edinburgh for our last few working years there, we had a surprise visit from the Ntarean, David Zac Niringiye. He had been in my last Confirmation class and has since been Bishop of Kampala. Coming to preach at a different school, he teased us mercilessly from the pulpit. Did we still have Open House, with the Coffee and the Biscuit? Indeed we did just as we had done in Mbarara, and would soon continue to do in London among international students, sometimes from over seventy nationalities.

Then when we did move to the British capital, three Ntareans soon searched us out and came to visit. What fun that was, but we thought it might be the last human contact with Ankole. Happily that was not so, for it continues even to this day in the wonderful fellowship of the Christian church already touched on. When we worship on Sundays we do so in the company of some who know Uganda well. Best of all, at present there is Dr Wilber Sabiti, together with his family, whose gracious wife was born on the once royal hill of Kamukuzi.

There are other anecdotes from that tragic year of 1972. It was July and term had ended. Here are a few more from the next couple of months. Our radios told us that Tanzanian troops were massing on the borders, all of which were now closed. Suspecting this might be right, but knowing not to believe everything in the media, we set out on a long planned holiday through Bukoba, across the lake to Kisumu (where with our Uganda number plates I was arrested as a spy) and (released after long interrogation) we went on to the Serengeti, down to the beaches at Mombasa, and then the long drive back through Kenya to stay with friends at St Andrew's, Turi. After some days we set off homewards, but on reaching Eldoret met with a stream of cars coming in the opposite direction. They contained many Europeans of various nationalities who flagged us down and told us to turn back. They were fleeing from Uganda.

So after further days at Turi, we resolved that we must all go back. The last thing for the Chaplain at Ntare to do in times of trouble was to scuttle away. We approached the border somewhat nervously, anticipating difficulties. Slowly I brought the car to within thirty yards of the Uganda frontier post, and then walked towards it to make myself known. To my astonishment, and the amazement of the family watching from the car, a soldier came running out to meet me, gave me a big hug, and said, "Thank you for coming back to Uganda!" A year before I had been teaching him in the Sixth Form at Ntare.

I could then tell of our ten days under house arrest while staying with friends at Kyambogo, during which the locals stayed "loyal" and supplied us all with food, while the British High Commission representative spread the word to "emulate the cockroach"; of my reconnaissance to Mbarara among a Ugandan army convoy; of my returning alone to collect the family, only to be engaged at the first of twelve road-blocks to carry a "captured Chinese machine from Mutakula" in the back of our "Beetle" and take it all the way to the then notorious Lubira Barracks; and of our final welcome back in Mbarara.

Then came Independence Day 1972. The previous month there had been this terrible slaughter in Mbarara following a failed attempt from Tanzania to topple the Amin regime. It was especially memorable as the Tenth such celebration. For some strange reason I had to dress in Anglican robes and sit with the Bishop among the notables on the platform for the parade outside the District Commissioner's Office. On my other side sat Major Juma, immaculately dressed, but a symbol of the current repression and brutality. I did not enjoy the experience, and was saddened that the euphoric proceedings contained no note of sorrow for any failings there might have been over the last decade. No human enterprise is ever free of them. It also caused me to record my feelings on that day. The following doggerel lines have no poetic merit, but they express the horror and the longing for deliverance felt by expatriates but even more so by most of the indigenous population of their country.

Tenth Anniversary of Uganda's Independence

Retrospect 1962:
Some spoke of the end of an Empire
and a cause that was lost.
Others saw only fulfilment –
the handing on a torch –
To whom it was always intended.

But twilight it was for all –
Whether prelude of glorious dawn, or
a dismal darkness.

Review 1972:
Ten years after, we are asked
to assess the achievement.
Much has been perpetuated,
sometimes after another manner;
Expansion and initiation
has formed part of the Progress;
And there has been loss.

But what is the gain-if fear?
What greater loss than security?
When will the killing end?

Is the longed for liberty,
more free, or less
than the 'years of bondage'?
And what of the 'years of blood'?

1966: and the *Kabaka* `
shelled out of a palace,
but he survived longer
than many a subject.

1969: 'Our President has been shot' –
but he was not
among the dead.

1971: when again the Exile survived
though many less exalted heads
were lost
in the 'bloodless revolution'.

1972: with new rains
came more blood,
in guerrilla invasions,
and greater still,
in the mopping up
which followed their extinction.

When will the killing end?
Will a mother yet dwell secure
with her children, and husband?

The twilight is over,
but we have forgotten the darkness.
which always comes
before a dawning.

Truly without understanding
were those who proclaimed the Sunrise,
When in the night
An old Flag fell
To the New –
which was also in Darkness.

At once, the evening stillness was not
wracked by storms,
but they have come.

Perhaps the tempest rages fiercest
in the moments before Day's break
and Calm will replace Terror:
Surely there is no worst befall
before the Light

But when will the killing end?
When breaks the true Dawn –
(how many false ones?)
Upon the people
and the Land
we love?

Hopefully that time has now come, and as long as human sin-
fulness is kept in check, it will endure.

However, this book is not supposed to contain my mem-
oirs, but a quite different story concerning others. So please
forgive the ramblings of age, and ignore them as you were invited to do at the start of this Appendix.

What a privilege to have such a rich fund of memories (so
many unrecorded) from Mbarara, in that land then so much
loved, with a better future so much longed for.

RELEVANT BOOKS
AND ARTICLES

(Numbers after each work refer to footnotes where they are mentioned, and pp.117–120 to notes a–ii printed there.)

Atlas of Uganda, Entebbe (1962), 285

Bamunoba, Y. K., "A Reconstruction of the History of the Church in Ankole', Makerere (1966/67), typescript, 206

Bamunoba, Y. K., 'Note on Islam in Ankole', *Dini na Mila*, Vol 1. no.2, (1965)

Berkeley, G. F. H., 'My recollections of Wellington College', quoted in Newsome, D. (see below).

Boase, F. *Modern English Biography*, Truro (1892), 75

Bouniol, J. *The White Fathers and their Mission*, London (1929), 244

Bulletin of the East Africa Study Circle, xi

Burke's Landed Gentry, London (1914), 136

Burke's Landed Gentry of Ireland, London (1958), 129, 133

Burton, R. F. *First Footsteps in East Africa*, London (1856), 76

Byaruhanga, C., *Bishop Alfred Tucker and the Establishment of the Native African Church*, Nairobi (2008), 7

Casati, G., *Ten years in Equatoria and the return with Emin Pasha*, London (English Translation 1891), viii

Clayton, H., (Trans.) *Matayo omu Lunyankole* (St Matthew's Gospel in *Runyankore*), London (1907), 253

Clayton, H., Owen, W. E., & Baker, M. T., (Trans,) *Yohana omu Lunyankole*, (St John's Gospel in *Runyankore*) London (1910), 253

Clayton Letters, in possession of the family

Colvile, H. E., *Land of the Nile Springs*, London (1895), 28, 40, 45, 284, 303, 308

Cook, A. R., Journal Letters 1899

Cook. A. R., 'The Future of the language of Bunyoro', CMS Archive

Cook, H. B., *A Doctor and his Dog in Uganda*, London (1903), 271

Cunningham, G. G., 'Description of the country passed through by the Ankole Expedition 1894 via King Ntale's Capital' [Report No. 2] in ESA, 293, 307

Cunningham, G. G., 'The Report of the Ankole Expedition' [Report No. 1] in ESA, 292

Cunningham, J. F., *Uganda and its Peoples*, London (1905), viii

Davis, M. B., *Lunyoro-Lunyankole-English and English-Lunyoro-Lunyankole Dictionary*, London, (1938), 260

Doornbos, M. R., *Regalia Galore: the Decline of Ankole kingship*, Nairobi (1975)

Doornbos, M. R., *Not all the King's Men: Inequality as a Political Instrument in Ankole*, The Hague (1978), 7

Doornbos, M. R., 'Stanley's Blood-Brotherhood' *UJ* 30/2 (1966), 20, 112, 184

Doornbos, M. R., *The Ankole Kingdom Controversy: Regalia Galore Revisted*, Kampala, (2001), 7

Drumkey's Year Book for East Africa, Bombay (1904), 82, 88

East Africa Standard Newspaper, Nairobi

East African Royal Commission Report 1953-55, HMSO 1955 (Cmd 9475), 11, 268

Elliot, G. F. Scott, *A Naturalist in mid Africa*, London, (1896), 35, 300, p.117.k

Ennis, G. F. and Carter, W. Morris, *Laws of the Uganda Protectorate in force on 31 December 1909*, Entebbe, (1910), 274

Flood, Dr W. E., 'The Early Cancellations of East Africa and Uganda' in *South African Philatelist*, (Februry 1956), 283

Foster, J., *Alumni Oxonienses 1715–1886*, London (1888), 78

Foster, W. D. *The Early History of Scientific Medicine in Uganda*, Nairobi, (1970), 135

Garstin, Sir W., *Report on the Drainage of the Upper Nile with proposals for the improvement of that river*, Cairo (1904), viii, 96, 148, 273

General Report on the Uganda Protectorate for the year ending 31 March 1904, London (1904), (Africa no. 12)

Gilbert, W. S. *The Bab Ballads*, London (1873), 42

Gorju, J. E., 'Diary of the Mbarara Mission' by Father (later Bishop) Gorju. Typescript, 249, 250 252

Gorju, J. E., *Essai de Grammaire Comparée - Du Ruganda au Runyoro au Runyankole,* Alger (1906)

Gorju, J. E., *Essai de Grammaire Runyankole*

Gray, Sir J. M., 'A History of Ankole' MS (1952), 16, 22, 26, 245, 309, p.117.j

Gray, Sir J. M. 'Anglo-German Relations in Uganda 1890-1892', *Journal of African History* 1/2 (1960), p.117.c

Gray, Sir J. M. 'Early Treaties in Uganda', *UJ* 12/1 (1948), p.116.b

Gresford Jones, H., *Uganda in Transformation*, London (1926)

Grimshaw, E. A., 'A Short History to the Vicariate of the Upper Nile', MS quoted in Gale, H. P. *Uganda and the Mill Hill Fathers*, London (1959), 246

Gugler, J., 'Urban Growth in sub-Saharan Africa, *Nkanga* no.6 (1956), 265, 269

Gutkind, P. C. W. 'Town life in Uganda' *UJ* 20 (1956), 267

Harrison, J. W. *Mackay of Uganda*, London (1890), 237

Hawes, H. W. R. (Ed), *Ebigano by'ebyabaireho Omuri Uganda,* (Stories from Uganda History) Longmans, (1965), 60

Hill, M. F., *Permanent Way*, Nairobi (1949), 37

Institute of Civil Engineers, *Minutes of Proceedings*, London, Vol. 179

Ingham, K., *The making of modern Uganda,* (1958), 287

Jack, E. M., *On the Congo Frontier*, London (1915), 8, 23, 95, 100, 107, 166, 167, 212

Johnston, H. H., *The Uganda Protectorate*, London (1902), viii, p.119.bb

Kaggwa, Sir A. *Basekabaka b'e Buganda*, English translation by Kiwanuka, M. S. M., Nairobi (1971), 110

Kagume, A. M., 'Church and Society in Ankole, Uganda', PhD University of Bristol (1993), 7, 14, 221–224

Kahigiriza, J., *Bridging the Gap*, Kampala (2001), 7, 185

Kamugungunu, L., & Katate, A. G., *Abagabe b'Ankole*, Dar-es-Salaam (1955), 24, 31, 60, 67, 69, 113

Karugire, S. R., *A history of Nkore in Western Uganda to 1896*, Oxford (1971), xiii, 13, 15, 19, 41, 66, 71, 93, 139, 154, 180, 181, 187, 305

Karugire, S. R., *Nuwa Mbaguta and the establishment of British rule in Ankole*, Kampala (1973), xiii, 4, 6, 174, 182, 183, 190, 212, 217, 227, 228

Katate, A. G. & Kamugungun, A G., *Abagabe b'Ankole*, Dar-es-Salaam (1956)

Kiepert, R., *Übersichtskarte der Expedition des Dr. Emin Pascha 1890-92*, (in Stuhlmann, below), p.117

Langheld, W., *Zwanzig Jahre in Deutschen Kolonnien*, Berlin (1909). 26, 309, p.117.j

Langlands, B. W., 'Early Travellers in Uganda', *UJ* 26/1 (1962), 270, 286, 291, (310), p.118.q

Leakey, R. H, *Church Missionary Intelligencer*, (1898), 194

Lowsley, L. D., 'Supplementary Annual Medical Report: Ankole District 1904', 125

Lugard, F. D., *The Rise of our East African Empire*, Edinburgh (1893), 33, 34, p.117.e

Lukyn Williams, F., 'Blood Brotherhood in Ankole' *UJ* 2/5 (1935), 21, 24,

Lukyn Williams, F., 'Early Explorers in Ankole' *UJ* 2/3 (1935), 32, 206, 288, 302

Lukyn Williams, F., 'Nuwa Mbaguta, Nganzi of Ankole', *UJ* 10/2 (1946), 212, 288, 305

Maari, E., 'The Growth of the Anglican Church in Ankole *c.*1899-1951', M.Phil Council for Academic Awards (1984), 7

Macallister, R. J. D., 'Report for Ankole June 1900' in ESA, p.119.y

Macallister, R. J. D., 'Report for Ankole August 1900' in ESA, 127

Maddox H. E. (Trans.), *Ekiragano Ekihyaka ekya Mukama waitu kandi Omujuni waitu Isa Masiya, Matayo omu Lunyankole,* (New Testament in *Runyoro-Rutoro),* London (1905)

Maddox, H. E. (Trans.), *Ekitabu Ekirukwera ekya Ruhanga ekibeta Baibul,* (Holy Bible in *Runyoro-Rutoro*) London (1912), 262

Mbaguta, N., 'The Words of the Hon. Nuwa Mbaguta – the "Katikiro"', possibly from *Munno,* February 1913 – see Gray, J. papers, *op. cit.,* 5, 65

Mengo Notes, II/VII, Kampala, (November 1901), 235

Millar, E., in *Uganda Notes,* (January 1913), 236

Moffat, R. U., 'PMO's Report 1903', Entebbe

Morris H. F., *A History of Ankole,* Nairobi (1962), 114, p.117.l

Morris, H. F., *The Heroic Recitations of the Bahima of Ankole,* Oxford (1964), 230

Morris, H. F., 'Some Aspects of Runyankore' *UJ* 22/1 (1958), 241

Morris, H. F., 'The Murder of H. St G. Galt' *UJ* 24/23, 1960

Morris, H. F. & Kirwan, B. E. R., *A Runyankore Grammar,* Kampala (1957), 248

Moyse-Bartlett, H., *The King's African Rifles,* Aldershot (1956) , 1, 2, 56, 123

Newsome, D., *Godliness and good-learning,* London (1961), 311

Nganwa, K. K., *Abakozire Eby'Okutangaaza Omuri Ankole* (Some Eminent People of Ankole), EALB (1948), 259

Ntare School History Society, 'The development of the town of Mbarara', typescript (1970), 124, 289, 302, 304

O'Connor, A. M., 'The distribution of towns in sub-Saharan Africa' in Gugler, J., 'Urban growth in sub-Saharan Africa', (*Nkanga* no. 6), 265, 272

Papers relating to the events in the Uganda Protectorate, London (1898) C.8941 (Africa no. 2)

Perham, M. & Bull, M., *The diaries of Lord Lugard*, London (1959), 32, p.117.e.f.g.

Perham, M., *Lugard The Years of Adventure 1858-98*, London (1956), 38

Phillips, C. J., 'The Postage Stamps of Uganda', *Stanley Gibbons Monthly Journal*, (February 1904), 281

Pilkington, G., 'A Three Year enterprise for Uganda' *Church Missionary Intelligencer*, May (1896), 191

Pirouet, M. M. L., *Black Evangelists: the Spread of Christianity in Uganda 1891-1914*, London (1978), based on PhD University of East Africa (1968), 188

Pirouet, M. M. L., 'Evangelists and sub-imperialists', *Dini na Mila*, Vol.4 no.1, October 1969.

Racey, R. R., 'Ankole District Report for October 1900' in ESA, 165, p.119.dd

Racey, R. R., 'Report for Ankole', February 1901' in ESA, p.120.ff

Racey, R. R., 'Report for Ankole', June 1901 in ESA, p.120.gg

Rapport Annuel (Year Book of the White Fathers' Mission), 251

Schweitzer, G., *The Life and Work of Emin Pasha*, London (1898). P.117.c.d

Scott Elliot, G. F., see under Elliot

Shaw, W. A., *The Knights of England*, London (1906)

Sitwell, C. G. H., 'Diary', in ESA, 52 55,

Stanley Gibbons Catalogues, 279

Stanley Gibbons Monthly Journal, (February 1904), 281

Stanley, H. M., *In Darkest Africa*, London (1890), 20, p.116.b

Stanley, H. M., *Through the Dark Continent*, London (1878), p.116.a

Stanley-Smith, A. C. *et al.*, (Trans.) *Baibuli Erikwera* (Holy Bible in *Runyankore-Rukiga*), 262

Stanley-Smith, A. C. *et al.*, (Trans.) *Endegaano Ensya* (New Testament in *Runyankore-Rukiga*), 253

Steinhart, E. L., *Conflict and Collaboration, the kingdoms of Western Uganda*, Princeton (1977), 7, 182

Steinhart, E. L., 'Primary Collaboration in Ankole 1891–1901 – an interpretation of the response to the colonial impact', Makerere U.E.A., SSC History Papers

Stock, E., *History of the C.M.S.*, London (1916), 189

Stuhlmann, F. *Mit Emin Pascha ins Herz von Afrika*, Berlin (1894), p.117.h

Stuhlmann, F., *Übersichtskarte der Expedition des Dr. Emin Pascha 1890-92* Gezeichnet von Dr. Richard Kiepert, p.117

Taylor, C., *A Simplified Runyankore-Rukiga Dictionary*, Kampala (1959), 261

Taylor, J. V., *The Growth of the Church in Buganda*, London (1958), 197

The Times Newspaper, London

Thomas, H. B., 'On the Frontiers of Another World, *UJ* 31/1 (1967)

Thomas, H. B. and Dale, I. R., 'Uganda Place Names: Some European Eponyms' *UJ* 17/2 (1953)

Thomas, H. B. & Spencer, A. E., *A History of the Uganda Lands and Surveys Department*, Entebbe (1938), p.117.i

Thomas, H. B., & Scott, R., *Uganda*, London (1938)

Tucker, A. R., 'A Missionary Journey Through Ankole', *Church Missionary Intelligencer*, (1900), 146

Tucker, A. R., *Eighteen Years in Uganda and East Africa*, London (1908), 197, 202, 203, p.118.w

Twaddle, M., 'The Founding of Mbale', *UJ* 30/1 (1966), 11

Uganda Handbook, Entebbe (1913), 98, 114, 172

Uganda Herald, 11 November 1942

Uganda Notes, January 1907

Uganda Notes, June 1902

Uganda Notes, August 1902

Uganda Protectorate Estimates, 1900–01, 120

Uganda Protectorate Estimates, 1901–02, 121

Vincent, W. T., *Records of the Woolwich District,* Woolwich (1888)

Weekes, D., *Ankole Religion and Christianity,* London (forthcoming), xi, xii, 18n, 29n, 91n, p.120.dd

Weekes, D., 'Cunningham's Journey through Ankole 1894', *UJ* 37 (1973), vii, ix, 29, 312

Weekes, D., 'John Macallister and the Town of Mbarara 1898-1900', *UJ* 37 (1973), vii, ix, 11, 74, p.118.p

Weekes, D., 'The Growth of Christianity in Nkore (Ankole) in Western Uganda before 1912', MTh University of Aberdeen (1979), xi

White Fathers, *Amakuru Mahango G'Edini omu Runyankole* (a simple Bible and Church History), Entebbe, (1927), 247

Willis, J. J., 'Journal', original in The Library, Lambeth Palace, London

Woodward, E. M., *Précis of information concerning the Uganda Protectorate,* London (1902), 306

Worsley, P. *The Third World,* London (1964), 6

Wright, M. A., *Buganda in the Heroic Age,* Nairobi (1971), 53, 175, 177

INDEX

37986875R00107

Made in the USA
Charleston, SC
23 January 2015